WHAT THEY DON'T TEACH YOU IN CATHOLIC COLLEGE

Other books by John Wijngaards

Biblical Spirituality

Jesus Forever: Fact and Faith

Inheriting the Master's Cloak

Background to the Gospels

Communicating the Word of God

Experiencing Jesus

God Within Us

My Galilee, My People

Academic

*The Ordination of Women in the Catholic Church:
Unmasking a Cuckoo's Egg Tradition*

The Gospel of John and His Letters

How to Make Sense of God

*The Dramatization of Salvific History
in the Deuteronomic Schools*

*Women Deacons in the Early Church:
Historical Texts and Contemporary Debates*

WHAT THEY DON'T TEACH YOU IN CATHOLIC COLLEGE

Women in the priesthood and the mind of Christ

John Wijngaards, DD, LSS

Acadian House
PUBLISHING
Lafayette, Louisiana, USA

Library of Congress Control Number: 2020910098

ISBN 10: 0-9995884-4-3
ISBN 13: 978-0-9995884-4-4

♦ Published by Acadian House Publishing, Lafayette, Louisiana
   (Edited by Trent Angers; editorial assistance and research by Madison Louviere)
♦ Design and pre-press production by Allison Nassans
♦ Printed by Sheridan Books, Chelsea, Michigan

*I dedicate this book
to my indomitable mother, Dietze van Hoesel,
and to my loving wife, Jackie Clackson.*

Acknowledgements

I gratefully acknowledge the contributions by my colleagues in the Wijngaards Institute for Catholic Research who over the decades have helped me to widen and deepen my research on and understanding of the questions surrounding women and the priesthood.

Foreword

Authorities in the Catholic Church continue to refuse to ordain women as deacons, priests or bishops. They attempt to blame Jesus Christ for this decision. It was Jesus, they say, who excluded women from Holy Orders, permanently.

I worked as a missionary in India for 20 years and saw with my own eyes how the lack of ecclesial authority ravaged a number of Christian denominations. I experienced how the Second Vatican Council imposed rapid, much-needed reforms on all Catholic communities: vernacular liturgies, a healthier management in religious congregations, a refreshing openness to other religions. I have seen the benefits of exercising control, believe me.

I respect the Church's teaching authority, and yet I know I have to speak out when it makes a mistake as it has done in the past. So in this book I will be direct and thorough as I address this issue that is so critical to the future of the Catholic Church.

This is all the more necessary because in the past four decades Rome has surrounded itself with dubious friends. There is a Dutch proverb that says "A true friend is the one who dares to correct me." Rome selected many bishops who agreed with its position on women in the priesthood. Rome appointed only advisors to its Vatican commissions who had passed "the loyalty test." Rome sanctioned academics who contradicted its views, resulting in scholars in Catholic institutions maintaining a diplomatic silence. That silence needs to be broken.

Women should be ordained priests. Though Jesus himself did not choose a woman among the original twelve apostles, having women serve as priests in our time is very much in harmony with *his mind*. It is what he would have wanted.

But how do we know the mind of Christ?

First, let's be aware that New Testament scholars have adopted the convention to distinguish "Jesus" from "Christ." I will do the same in this book. When we speak of "Jesus" we refer to the carpenter from Nazareth who preached the Kingdom of God, a good man who was driven to his death by his Jewish opponents under the Roman governor Pontius Pilate. "Christ" stands for the risen Jesus, the man now recognised to be the Son of God, the person who emerges as the transcendent mediator in world Christianity. "Jesus" and "Christ" are not two separate individuals. They are one and the same person. They represent two stages in the evolution of that person.

It makes sense to distinguish between "Jesus" and "Christ" when it comes to discussing the ordination of women as priests. We can ask two distinct questions:

Did Jesus envisage women in spiritual leadership functions?

Does Christ want women to be admitted to the priesthood now?

As we shall see, answers to these questions overlap to a great extent, but it is still worthwhile considering them one after the other.

When someone is still alive, it is easy. We can ask him or her to explain what precisely he or she has in mind. After a person has died, it becomes much more difficult. Sometimes we can determine his or her mind by uncovering explicit or implicit decisions in the person's own life. At times we have only *pointers* to help us to understand.

To determine "the mind of Jesus" on the matter of the ordination of women, we should explore three questions:

• Are there *pointers* in his life that show Jesus would have been open to women ministering as priests?

• Did Jesus at any time *explicitly rule out* women's taking part in the ordained ministries?

• Did Jesus make *implicit decisions* that show he wanted women to be included in the ministry?

And, what's more, Jesus was not just a human founder. He poured his own Spirit into us. He promised that in future eras the Spirit would reveal his mind to us.

St. John's Gospel contains collections of Jesus' teaching which the author brought together in Jesus' sermons at the Last Supper. These sermons reflect on Christian life in future periods to come, how Christ will remain present to us. The overriding theme is God's love, how it will pervade our lives, and how it should saturate our relationships. Though Jesus will no longer be there, he will as Christ continue to guide us through his Spirit. Jesus made this commitment:

> I will ask the Father, and he will send you someone else as Counsellor to be with you forever, that Spirit of Truth whom the world can never receive since it neither sees nor knows him; but you know him, because he is with you, he is in you.

Christ's Spirit in us is a *parakletos*, an advisor, a counsellor. The meaning of the term has been explained in many ways by the Fathers of the Church and theologians; it designates Christ's Spirit as a teacher, an interpreter.

"In years to come," Christ says, "I will remain with you through my Spirit in you. The Spirit will make everything clear." This promise is confirmed in these verses from the Gospel of John:

> I have said these things to you while still with you. But the Counsellor, the Holy Spirit, whom the Father will send in my name, will teach you everything and remind you of everything I have said to you.

> I still have many things to say to you but they would be too much for you now. When the Spirit of Truth comes he will lead you to the fullness

of truth, since he will not be speaking as from himself but will say only what he has learnt *[from me]*; he will explain to you things that lie in the future.

According to John's Gospel, therefore, Christ's Spirit in our hearts acts as an advisor and interpreter who helps us to understand what Jesus would have wanted within the new circumstances of the future. This is a crucial insight that is emphasized in the Gospel of John. In Jesus's lifetime he could not do justice to all the developments that would occur in the future. There certainly were demands and challenges that could not be foreseen or understood by the first disciples. But, because we Christians carry Christ's Spirit in our hearts, we would know what to do. The Spirit within us would disclose what Christ expected of us in the new situation.

The Spirit has indeed revealed Christ's mind, and it is clear that women should be welcomed into the Catholic priesthood.

– *John Wijngaards*

Preface

In the mid-1970s, I wrote a book titled *Did Christ Rule Out Women Priests?* The book was in response to *Inter Insigniores* (translated: Among the most significant...), which was issued in 1976 by the Congregation for the Doctrine of the Faith.

Since then much has changed: The Vatican has upped its rhetoric, and much additional serious research has been done to shed light on the critically important subject of women in the priesthood. This book is much more than an update: It throws the net wider, it digs deeper, it lays bare the real issues.

On the following pages, I will attempt to answer the key questions surrounding the matter of women in the priesthood.

To begin with: What about *the fact* itself? Why are women not ordained priests in the Catholic Church? Church authorities say it was Jesus himself who ruled them out, and this can be proved from Tradition (Chapter 2 and 3; Appendix 1).

However, academic studies prove conclusively that the real culprit has been cultural prejudice. It was ancient bias against women assuming leadership positions that caused their exclusion (Chapter 3).

Moreover, it is clear that Jesus never meant his choice of just men for the twelve apostles to establish a permanent rule (Chapter 4).

Are there *pointers* in the Gospel texts that show Jesus would not be against women taking on leadership roles? The answer is yes, there are. Jesus' respect for women shows he would not oppose their full participation in Holy Orders (Chapter 5 and 6).

Did Jesus make an *implicit decision* that demonstrates he would be open to women in the ministry? Yes, he did. Jesus instituted a new priesthood open to all through baptism and love (Chapter 7).

And at the Last Supper Jesus commissioned both men and women to celebrate the Eucharist in his memory. In this way he also implicitly empowered women to preside at the Eucharist (Chapter 8).

And what does *the Spirit* reveal to us about Christ's mind? Church authorities themselves sacramentally ordained women as deacons, and in some cases even as priests (Chapter 9).

Throughout nearly two millennia the faithful have already believed some women fully shared in Christ's priesthood – including Jesus' mother Mary – and they confirm the same belief today (Chapter 10).

It is clear that the Church has made mistakes in the past, including its condoning of slavery, and was painfully slow to correct this error. The Church is also mistaken on the issue of ordaining women and should act now to facilitate their entry into the priesthood. (Chapter 11).

It is time for the Church to listen to what Jesus Christ really wants (Chapter 12).

– J.W.

Table of Contents

Introduction

Faith, reason and women
in the Catholic priesthood

Leaders of the Roman Catholic Church have
been adamant in their opposition to women in
the priesthood, particularly since the 1970s. They
vigorously defend the status quo even when their
arguments don't seem to hold up to rigorous
examination from the standpoint of faith or reason.

They've gone to great lengths to express their
views on the matter and to suppress opposing views
within Catholic institutions. It's company policy.
One Pope, John Paul II, went so far as to declare
in foreboding tones that the decision to exclude
women from the priesthood is final, that the case
is closed.

But there are those who beg to differ – and they
hail from virtually every continent on earth.

Surely the case is not closed so long as the Holy
Spirit continues to prompt men and women of good
faith to press the issue, to stay with it, to continue
advocating for change until the best interest of the
Church is served.

Commentators on the Eternal Word Television
Network (EWTN) speak of women in the priesthood
only in the most negative and disparaging of terms.
Their attitude on the matter seems to be company

policy. It's a taboo subject, never to be advocated in Catholic seminaries. And the Vatican surely doesn't allow it to be taught in Catholic colleges.

There's an old saying about how, when in Rome, priests and seminarians are advised to behave if they want to stay in the good graces of the higher-ups. This advice is especially applicable when it comes to touchy subjects:

When in Rome, don't think too much.

If you must think, don't speak.

If you must speak, don't write.

If you must write, don't publish.

If you must publish, don't sign.

Now, this admonition has been around for ages, and women's ordination is one of the issues to which it applies. It's a sure bet that anyone anywhere in the world who wears a Roman collar is expected to avoid this subject, and certainly never to discuss it in favorable terms.

Clearly, many priests today hold to the men-only viewpoint because that's the Church's age-old tradition. And besides, they believe, from what they've read and heard, that's the way Jesus intended it to be. But, the truth is, that never was Jesus's intention, as the evidence on the following pages will show.

Indeed, the author of this book, John Wijngaards, DD, LSS, started from the same traditionalist position as most other priests and then discovered material that changed his mind and heart on the matter. He has since grown into one of the most ardent and knowledgeable advocates for women in the priesthood. He has spent literally half his life conducting in-depth research on the subject and writing about it. Being an easy-to-follow teacher, he has written quite a number of books and booklets on this topic; he's given lectures, written newspaper and magazine articles, made videos, and set up online courses. He also supervised the establishment of a website, www.womenpriests.org, which is said to be "the largest online academic library on this topic in the world."

In 1983, he founded the Wijngaards Institute for Catholic Research, which is headquartered in London and is at the forefront of the worldwide movement to include women in the priesthood. An internationally renowned theologian and Scripture scholar, he always presents a compelling case for the ordination of women, as he does on the following pages. The genesis of his involvement in this issue is revealed in one of the chapters herein.

Dr. Wijngaards is a former vicar general of the Mill Hill Missionaries of the UK. Like a number of priests throughout the Western World, he resigned from the priestly ministry because of the Church's refusal to ordain women. Since then, since 1998, he has spent much of his life uncovering more and more evidence in support of women in the priesthood. He generously shares his research, reasoning and life experiences in this book, calling upon leaders of the Church to step out in faith and reason and to open the door to the ordination of women.

* * * * *

The institutional Church and many of the main men in Rome maintain that Jesus never intended for women to be priests, that He established a permanent norm for the priesthood when He appointed only men to be apostles. The hierarchy doesn't like to acknowledge the pivotal, indisputable point that Jesus's decision was made in light of the cultural norms of the day – 2,000 years ago. It was, at the time, a world dominated by men, and it remained so for centuries.

But that time has passed. It's long gone. The culture in which we live today is our own. The exclusion of women from the priesthood is a relic of the past.

By refusing to ordain women, the Church continues to deprive the laity of a grace that is rightly theirs. The Church today clings to the way of an ancient culture, partly out of fear of breaking with tradition.

But, for some, the central questions about Jesus's intentions remain. At the last Supper, when He said, "Do this in memory of me," was he intending to exclude the female disciples who were in the room – even though He said, "Take this *all* of you"? Is there any way to honestly and reliably figure out whether Jesus would have wanted women in

xix

the priesthood in our time? These questions are answered thoroughly in this book. The answers, when read with an open mind, should remove the doubts that have paralyzed the thinking of the Church hierarchy on this issue for generations.

* * * * *

Having women in the ranks of the Catholic priesthood surely would enrich the ministry – and the Church as a whole. Generally speaking, are women not naturally more nurturing, more empathetic than men? Is not their approach to problem-solving more patient and gentle, and perhaps less confrontational?

In priestly ministry, as in communication in general, the effectiveness of the effort is determined in no small measure by *who* is doing the ministering. It is determined not only by his or her knowledge of matters of faith and morals, but also by his or her empathy and compassion, his or her relatability.

Since the Church is considered to be "the mystical body of Christ," and since it is comprised of far more female members than males, would the Church not be better served to include female priests, who may be better able to relate to the female majority? Without a doubt, women can relate to other women in ways a man never could. And, of course, the converse is true as well.

Moreover, since the Church has held traditionally that a call to the priesthood truly is a call from

God, who among us mere mortals would have the authority to argue definitively that such an invitation cannot apply to a woman? If a woman announces she has heard God's call to serve the Church as a priest, should she be told that she must have misunderstood? Or that she simply has an over-active imagination?

* * * * *

Now, if women's ordination were a matter of faith or morals, then the past Popes' pronouncements on the matter could be considered infallible – and the case would indeed be closed. But such is not the case. A men-only priesthood is merely an ancient tradition, a holdover from the Middle Ages and earlier.

It usually takes a while, but any number of traditions in the Church have been cast aside as no longer useful or practical; others have been abandoned because they were recognized as ill-informed or flawed, to put it mildly. For example, the Church no longer holds to the tradition of condoning slavery, though it rationalized the practice for well into the 19th century. The tradition of the Latin language Mass has been replaced, so that the laity can now understand what is being said at the altar. And we have long rejected the antiquated though traditionally held notion that only Roman Catholics can be saved – even though

15th century Pope Eugene IV asserted this idea in an official statement he issued in 1442.

The tradition of a male-only priesthood is one that no longer serves the best interest of the Church, if it ever did. Indeed, the majority of Catholics in the Western World are in favor of women's ordination. They see the need. They see the shortage of priests.

Let's face it, our Church isn't doing so well these days. It's past time for an infusion of new life. The ranks of the priesthood are shrinking. Fewer and fewer men are entering the seminaries. Sunday collections are down, as is attendance at Mass. A number of dioceses have declared bankruptcy due to heavy payouts in settlements in the infamous sexual abuse scandal. The rock-solid respect for the Church's authority has eroded in many quarters.

The Church is in need of rebuilding. The army of good men in Roman collars is in need of reinforcements.

Many find it inconceivable that Christ, in the Great Commission, would have directed his apostles to "go out and teach all nations" – but leave half the potential workforce behind! It defies logic that the Lord would have asked them to go out and evangelize the *whole* world using only *half* of the workers. Indeed, He had made it clear previously how He felt about halfhearted efforts, about lukewarm measures.

* * * * *

When Francis of Assisi was near the beginning of

his conversion from a life of debauchery and glory-seeking, he knelt before the crucifix in the chapel of San Damiano, in humility and submission, and prayed that the Lord might lead him down the right road. And he heard the voice of Christ, whether audibly or speaking to his heart:

"Rebuild my church, which is falling into ruin."

These words are thought of today as a mantra by many Franciscans and others who have the Church's best interests at heart. The message can be interpreted not only as an instruction to Francis in his day, but also to others who would serve the Church in the same generous spirit as Francis did in the 13th century. For many, a major component of rebuilding the Church is working to see the day when women are welcomed with open arms into the Catholic priesthood.

John Wijngaards is one such worker who is completely devoted to the cause, as can be seen on the following pages.

– *Trent Angers, OFS*
(Secular Franciscan Order)

WHAT THEY
DON'T TEACH
YOU IN
CATHOLIC
COLLEGE

A Church in need of reform

"Christ summons the Church to continual reformation as she goes her pilgrim way here on earth. The Church is always in need of reform, in so far as she is an institution of human beings here on earth. Thus if, in various times and circumstances, there have been deficiencies in moral conduct or in church discipline, or even in the way that church teaching has been formulated – to be carefully distinguished from the deposit of faith itself – these can and should be set right at the opportune moment."

– Vatican II, *Ecumenism*, No. 6

Chapter 1

The discovery and the shock

My world changed when I realized my own
preconceived, ill-informed notions
about the roles of women.

I remember the incident as if it happened only yesterday: a fleeting encounter that inadvertently showed my cultural bias regarding women and their potential for professional achievement.

This minor, though embarrassing episode occurred more than half a century ago, in a less-enlightened age than we live in today. I confess, I and most everyone I knew back then had a certain preconceived, ill-informed notion about women in the workplace.

At the time, in 1962, I was a young priest studying in Rome to obtain my doctorate in theology, and during the summer months I volunteered to do pastoral work in West Germany. Parish institutions there had come under enormous strain from the influx of hundreds of thousands of Catholics who came fleeing from East Germany.

On a particularly warm summer morning, I was helping out in a primary school run by the parish in the town of Osterode. Standing near the entrance to the school, I was chatting with parents who were dropping off their children. A Volkswagen stopped not far from me. A tall, middle-aged woman stepped out of the car, her shining black hair cascading down her shoulders. Holding a young boy at her side, she gave me a hand-written note: "Please allow my son to stay at home today. We are celebrating his granddad's sixtieth birthday." The note was signed by "Prof. Dr. C. J. Müller" (or something similar).

"Tell Professor Müller it's OK!" I told her, presuming the professor was her husband.

"I *am* Professor Müller," she replied, her Germanic-blue eyes probing my face.

Stammering my apologies, I expressed the hope that her family would enjoy a memorable celebration.

That evening, I used my daily examination of conscience exercise to reflect on the incident. What had happened? I had taken for granted that a professor would not have been a woman. True, female professors at universities were not so common in those days. Still, I had under-valued her and felt I was in the wrong for having done so. I felt all the more guilty because I was conscious of the fact that my mother, who I knew would have been quite capable of an academic career, had never been given the chance to attend university. She was the eldest of nine children. And while all five of her brothers had been sent for higher studies, the four girls were expected to survive by finding a suitable husband.

I realised then and there that I had to open my eyes and widen my mind.

Discovering women's full potential

The emancipation of women in Western societies had begun more than a century earlier. But it was only in the 1960s and '70s that it began to blossom. I say *began* because it was still far from perfect. Yes, women had received the right to vote. However, by 1970 only 13 women had won a seat in the 435-member U.S. Congress – compared to 127 nearly 50 years later, by 2019. In Great Britain in 1970, the 650-member House of Commons counted only two dozen women among their ranks; that number would swell to 220 by 2019.

Those who have not lived through the past 50 years, as I have, may have missed the mounting momentum of women making their mark on the nation's politics – through women ministers, women journalists, women leading political parties, even women prime ministers like Margaret Thatcher.

The same applies to other spheres of life in the Western world. Women medical doctors expanded from a few to being nearly half the workforce. Female lawyers claimed a 4% share in the 1970s and are now at 37%. Women occupied 7% of faculty positions at universities then, and now it's close to half. In the course of time, more and more women were appointed as financial experts in banks, magistrates and judges in law courts, board members of major corporations, you name it. Not complete emancipation yet, but an expanding massive presence in the leadership forces that drive our civil society. In 1951, women were still barred from reading the news on BBC TV. Now female presenters practically dominate the media.

The process has been one of our society gradually discovering women's potential. It has been a process of scales falling from people's eyes: recognising the error of cultural bias, false beliefs, mistaken assumptions, unproven preconceptions, and pure prejudice. It demanded a change in legislation and social attitudes.

Early girls' schools prepared girls for their future roles as wives and mothers and taught only religion, singing, dancing and literature. Now girls are taught alongside boys in comprehensive schools. They often surpass the male students in academic distinction. Moreover, legislation now tries to ensure that women are given equal opportunities in every respect.

A friend of mine, Mary Dittrich, now 90-plus years old, told me that in the 1930s she studied theology at Fribourg University in Switzerland. The faculty was run by Dominicans. She was the only woman in her class. The other students, being men, obtained Master's degrees. Mary, however, did not, even though she scored higher marks in her final exams than many of her fellow students. University rules forbade that academic degrees be awarded to a woman! Now more than half that university's graduates and a good number of professors are female.

"I was born too early," Mary commented ruefully. "But at least things are changing for the better."

The process of emancipation also involved women themselves. They, too, began to open their eyes and believe in undreamed new careers. As research showed in the 1970s, most girls in high schools saw their capabilities limited to history, literature and art – certainly not extending to the male domains of science and engineering. Now many women excel as scientists and engineers.

We all know there has been opposition to women's emancipation from conservative forces. In fact, much of it is still alive. An enormous amount still needs to be done. But, on the whole, Western societies now fully support *the principle* of genuine equality for women.

The full response to women's emancipation

In 1965, I began working in southern India. Apart from being a professor of theology and Sacred Scripture at St. John's Major Seminary in the city of Hyderabad, I had also become moderator of the conference of female religious, in the State of Andhra Pradesh. At that time, 1,800 religious sisters belonging to 20 or more congregations ran many vital institutions in the State: 40 hospitals, 550 schools and colleges, 55 hostels for boys and girls, as well as 10 homes for the elderly. Some sisters had obtained academic degrees in education or medicine. The vast majority, however, were woefully uneducated.

I was horrified, for instance, when visiting a novitiate in a small village, to learn that the novices were taught only the rules of their congregation and some basic skills such as cooking and nursing. The psalms at Lauds and Vespers were recited in Latin, even though these young women could understand only the Telugu language. Once a week the local Italian parish priest would give them a pep talk. He was a magnificent old-style missionary, but sadly out of date and not qualified to provide these future sisters with the knowledge of church history, doctrine, morality, spirituality and liturgy they would need.

I found it all quite distressing. I felt it my duty to step up and try to help somehow.

In line with the requirements of the Second Vatican Council, I put pressure on provincial superiors to upgrade the teaching provided to novices and juniors. In the case of so-called "local congregations," such as the St. Anne Sisters, I prevailed on their local bishops to send promising members of these orders to Rome for theological study. I also founded an institute in Hyderabad that was dedicated to providing year-long theological courses for junior sisters. Furthermore, I commissioned books on women's rights in our Telugu-language communication center. So, I was, in my own way, promoting women's emancipation. But I had not yet discovered the full extent of the challenge, nor its potential.

The Second Vatican Council had opened the possibility of creating new ministries for the laity. By 1974, various countries in Latin America had begun to introduce innovative functions for the apostolate in vast parishes, such as "a hosting committee" that welcomed newcomers, "visitors for the sick," "first communion educators," and so on. In India, we were used to village catechists who gave instructions and presided over prayer sessions.

But should more be done? It was decided to organise an All-India Seminar on New Ministries, to be held in June 1975. I was asked to do some research on possible new ministries for women. I relished the opportunity and began immediately.

A cursory reading of a passage in the classic commentary on Sacred Scripture by seventeenth-century theologian Cornelius a Lapide, S. J. , raised a big question to me: Could women be ordained *priests?*

I was shocked by the reasons which a Lapide gave for utterly rejecting this possibility; they were totally inadequate. I asked myself: What *are* the real reasons that rule out women? Finding good answers to this question would require extensive research, so I resolved to put in the necessary time – regardless of how long it would take. Since we possessed only a small collection of theological works in Hyderabad seminary, I made the 8-hour journey by train to Pune, where I was given access to the well-endowed library of the *Papal Athenaeum*, run by Jesuits. The German librarian even entrusted me with a key to the library so that I could work there day and night, if I so wished.

My findings in all the classical handbooks confirmed my suspicion. The exclusion of women was based on prejudice, not on any solid doctrinal ground. I wrote down the reasons, more or less in the order of importance given to them in medieval sources:

• Women are not created in God's image, as men are.

- Women are inferior in nature.
- Women are created to serve men.
- Paul forbade women to teach.
- Women's monthly menstrual periods would defile the sanctuary.
- Christ did not choose a woman among the twelve apostoles.
- Women are not complete human beings and therefore cannot represent Christ.

And this is not the complete list.

I also discovered that classic scholars John Middleton and Duns Scotus ruled women out of Holy Orders because women were, by Church law, forbidden to touch sacred objects. This brought to mind an incident my mother had related to me some years earlier, while I was studying for the priesthood.

It happened in the late 1930s in Surabaia, Indonesia, where I was born. My father was head of two Catholic primary schools there. Our parish priest, a Dutch Carmelite, frequently visited my parents in our home. One evening, while sitting down in the lounge with them, he pulled a guilded chalice from his bag and put it on the table in front of them.

"See!" he said. "This is our latest gift from the Netherlands."

My mother instinctively reached out, grabbed the chalice, and lifted it to admire it more closely.

"Oh, Mrs. Wijngaards, what are you doing?!" the priest called out. "Stop! You're a woman. You're not allowed to touch a sacred vessel! The law of the Church forbids it!"

"I put the chalice down, embarrassed and angry," my mother told me. "How ridiculous! A piece of metal being more sacred than a woman! I've never forgotten the humiliation."

And she was right, of course. It brought home to me with full force the implication of my findings on women's ordination. I saw it now: Women had been denied access to Holy Orders for the utterly crazy and unchristian reason that they were considered second-rate, substandard, dirty, you name it. It made my blood boil.

I knew that from that moment on it would be my duty as a theologian to explore the whole background further and expose the error of refusing priestly ordination to women.

Chapter 2

The truth comes clearer

Having women in the priesthood would greatly
increase the positive impact that the Universal
Church has on the world.

My research into the question of women's
ordination went on for several days as I
pored over multiple volumes in the Jesuit library in
Pune. And I experienced quite an awakening as I
pondered my own role in this weighty matter.

To begin with, how was it possible that during
all those long years of training in the seminary and
my four years' study at Roman universities, it had
never occurred to me to question *why* women could
not be ordained? I had just taken it for granted,
like everyone else I knew. And, besides, this is
one of those things they don't teach in Catholic
seminaries.

Even as moderator of all those dedicated religious sisters in southern India, the thought that some of them might have a priestly vocation had never struck me! I had been aware of the inadequate education afforded to most of the sisters, but their potential as full-fledged priests in the pastoral ministry had never come to mind. It had been a blind spot for me, as well as for practically the whole Catholic community.

My eyes were now open and I began to see a much wider horizon.

During those nights in Pune, I reflected on the difference it would make if women, too, could be invited to Holy Orders. For one thing, the sisters running hospitals could do more than provide medical care. As chaplains, some of them would be able to hear confessions, give the last sacraments, celebrate Mass in hospital chapels. And in all those small religious communities working in far-away villages, instead of just organising prayer services with Holy Communion on Sundays, they could have the full Eucharist. In fact, women priests would offer hope to the many parishes that struggled week after week to deal with 30 to 40 out-stations. The shortage of priests could be greatly alleviated if women could join the ranks of the priesthood.

The presence of female priests would also benefit the emancipation of women in general. What better message of true equality could be presented to girls than by showing them women operating as priests on an equal footing with men?

How would Jesus respond to all this?

I was sure – and I remain confident today – that he would welcome the ordination of women with open arms. He would want women to know that he values them as much as he values any man. And if even an ordinary priest like myself, with my limited pastoral experience, could see the vast potential for women joining the priestly ministry, then surely Jesus could see it even more clearly and would rejoice in the new vistas it would open.

* * * * *

While still in Pune, I pondered my latest mind-boggling discovery: that Jesus surely would welcome women priests. I discussed it at breakfast with Father Engelbert Zeitler. He was Provincial of the Divine Word Fathers. He had offered me accommodation at his own headquarters during my week-long stay in Pune.

"That's great news!" he said. "Yes, it makes sense. In a way, I'm not surprised. Well, explain your findings to the bishops. They should take up the matter with Rome."

"What I don't understand," I said, "is that Jesus has allowed women to be under-valued in that way for the last 2,000 years.... You'd think he should have intervened somehow, clarified matters. It's a bit like with slavery."

"What do you mean?" Fr. Zeitler asked.

"Well, for at least a thousand years Pope after Pope condoned slavery. They taught that keeping slaves, buying them, selling them is according to God's will. But the Second Vatican Council now teaches that 'every form of slavery is against the mind of Christ.' So, if it was against his mind, why did he put up with all those millions of poor men and women being captured in Africa and forced to work on American estates for all those years?" I asked.

"The Church is human," Fr. Zeitler responded. "Christ wanted it to be human. Its fate is in *our* hands. He puts up with our blindness and blunders. But cheer up. Times are changing. The Vatican Council declared that the Church needs constant reform. It started a new era. In the past, Catholics believed only baptised persons would be saved. Now the Church has acknowledged there are valuable elements in all religions. Traditionalists tried to hang on to Latin as the universal liturgical language. The Church has now sanctioned the use of the vernacular everywhere. I am sure within a few years we will see the first women admitted to the diaconate, then to the priesthood."

* * * * *

A few months after my discussion with Fr. Zeitler, in 1975, I sent a lengthy recommendation to the Indian Bishops' Conference. After describing how the "social myth of male superiority" had barred women from Holy Orders, I set out the reasons why they could and should be ordained. I suggested that after preparing the faithful for the change, the bishops should open the ministry of the diaconate to women. They should also begin to ordain some women as priests "for apostolic tasks that can be fulfilled only by them." I concluded with these words:

> What seems unacceptable at first may prove to be the will of Christ. What may seem unusual and strange may well be the demand of the Gospel in our own times. The pharisees rejected the Carpenter from Nazareth. They refused to recognize him as their priest when they stood under his cross on Calvary.
>
> The idea that a woman could express the priesthood of Christ may seem equally upsetting – and our prejudice as equally mistaken – as that of Jesus' pious contemporaries. Only honest appraisal in the light of Christ's Spirit should decide the question on women's ministry; not convention or personal fancy.
>
> After all, it is *Christ's* priesthood, not ours, we are speaking about.

What I did not know at the time was that in those same years the American Lutheran Church, the Episcopalian Church, the Anglican Church in Great Britain and other churches were making the first serious moves towards ordaining women. This develoment alarmed conservatives in the Vatican.

In January 1975, Pope Paul VI tried to suppress a report by the Pontifical Biblical Commission that had come to the same conclusion I had, namely that there were no valid reasons to exclude women from Holy Orders. In November of the same year he suppressed a similar report by the Working Group on the Ordination of Women set up by ARCIC (the Anglican/Roman Catholic International Consultation) that had met in Assisi. At the same time the Pope wrote a letter to the Archbishop of Canterbury setting out his opposition to the ordination of women. Then, in October 1976, he signed *Inter Insigniores*, the Declaration against the Admission of Women to the Ministerial Priesthood.

The Pope's verdict came as a shock to me and to many others. It was obvious to me that the Church's negative attitude to women was based on unmitigated cultural bias.

How could the Church attempt to reiterate and justify this bias just when the rest of the world was getting rid of it?

Rome's position

Through the decades that followed, the Vatican kept repeating its opposition to admitting women to the priesthood. (See Appendix 1 for excerpts from the various papal documents in question.) Pope John Paul II used especially strong language:

"In virtue of my ministry of confirming the brethren (cf. Lk 22:32) I declare that the Church has no authority whatsoever to confer priestly ordination on women and that this judgment is to be definitively held by all the Church's faithful."

The teaching of popes has to be taken seriously, of course. On the other hand, the use of strong language does not by itself mean that popes cannot be mistaken. For example, Pope Boniface VIII stated in 1302:

"There are two powers in the world, spiritual and temporal, the temporal subject to the spiritual... all under the divine authority entrusted to Peter and his successors.... Therefore we declare, we proclaim, we define that for every human creature it is absolutely necessary for salvation to be subject to the Roman Pontiff."

Then there was Pope Eugene IV's stunning declaration in 1442:

"The Holy Roman Church firmly believes, professes and preaches that no-one remaining outside the Catholic Church, not only pagans, but also Jews, heretics or schismatics, can become partakers of eternal life; but they will go to the 'eternal fire prepared for the Devil and his angels'.... No-one can be saved, even if he sheds his blood for Christ, unless he remains in the bosom of the Catholic Church."

But back to women in the priesthood ... If recent popes have opposed it so strongly, what are the reasons they gave for excluding women?

In short, it comes to this: *It is Jesus himself who decided only men should be priests. Through the centuries the Church has faithfully transmitted and implemented what he wanted. As Jesus had decreed, women were never ordained priests. This is part of Church doctrine. Church authorities in our own day cannot change a norm laid down by Jesus.*

How do we know what Jesus wanted?

We know it mainly from *Tradition*, the Vatican says. Scripture by itself does not give us a conclusive verdict on Jesus' will regarding women in the priesthood; we can know Jesus' decision with certainty only because of its constant and universal support in tradition, the Vatican maintains. Commentary on Pope Paul VI's *Inter Insigniores* of 1976 attempts to explain the Vatican's position in these words:

> We must not expect the New Testament *on its own* to resolve in a clear fashion the question of the possibility of women acceding to the priesthood.... It is an undeniable fact that the constant tradition of the Catholic Church has excluded women from the episcopate and the priesthood.... In the light of that tradition, then, it seems that the essential reason moving the Church to call only men to the sacrament of Orders and to the strictly priestly ministry is her intention to remain faithful to the type of ordained ministry willed by the Lord Jesus Christ.

But wait a minute! Is the Vatican not confusing Sacred Tradition with human tradition, that is, with *human* preferences and customs?

Chapter 3

Cultural prejudice
and social myth

For nearly 20 centuries, Christianity has been in the
grip of the ancient social myth of women's inferiority.

Why did the Catholic Church not ordain women in the past? Rome maintains it was Jesus who excluded them, and that he did so intentionally.

However, close study tells a completely different story.

To put it bluntly, women were discarded as second-rate, inadequate, inferior. Academic studies over the past decades have clearly established that the position of women in Christian communities ultimately was determined by prevailing cultural bias. Religious leadership by women was not compatible with patriarchal dominance in society.

In our own day, no one can deny the competence of women as doctors, lawyers, scientists, professors, you name it. But not so long ago women were not admitted to college studies. It is only since the 1870s that universities in North America and Europe gradually, very gradually, began to open their doors to female students.

Among the many people around the world who were shocked to learn the depth and breadth of the Church's ingrained prejudices against women was Catharina Halkes (1920-2011). I got to know her in the 1980s while she was gaining recognition as a highly respected theologian in the Netherlands. A delightful and very intelligent woman, she told me this story:

"From when I was young, I realized that women were underprivileged. For instance, I married in 1950, when for any legal transaction I still needed my husband's signature. Just imagine! Dutch law relaxed only in 1956, allowing married women to sign documents in their own right.

"In the beginning, while looking after my three children, as a sideline I obtained teachers' degrees in English language and Dutch literature. I gave private tutoring in the evening.

"When Vatican II started, I began to focus more on the restrictive practices in the Church. Only in 1972, when I was 52 years old, did the full connection between the women-hostile prejudices of society and the Church's ingrained patriarchy suddenly dawn on me. I reeled under the impact. It changed the course of my life!"

* * * * *

The factors that have shaped the different roles of men and women in society are partly genetic, partly social. Man and woman are physically different and this predisposes them to different tasks. However, as far as leadership and domination go, these have been determined mostly by the *common expectations of society*. A society floats on its "social myth," that is, on the cultural framework by which it lays down its objectives and norms of behaviour. It is that social myth that has in many regards dictated the fate of men and women.

Academic studies overwhelmingly point to *cultural prejudice* being the reason for women's past inferior status in society and in religion. This also applies to women's exclusion from the priesthood. The evidence identifies cultural prejudice as the culprit. It's plain to see that it is Greco-Roman gender bias that has heavily influenced so-called Christian "Tradition." But let's put this fact into perspective.

The 'social myth' of male superiority in Greco-Roman societies

When certain values have been accepted by a society, they tend to be strengthened over the course of time by the development of a "myth" through which these values are justified.

In traditional India, for instance, many people were convinced that the so-called castes embody higher or lower forms of human nature. The division of society into priests, warriors, merchants, farmers and outcasts was strengthened by a similar division of functions among the gods. Belief in the possibility of rebirth into higher or lower forms of life according to merit; ancient tales of superior races; superstitious preference for certain bodily traits, such as light skin – all these confirm the acceptance of inequality. Untouchability, restricting marriage to within the caste, and the observance of dietary rules peculiar to each caste – all these factors formed a web of convictions and practices that maintained the distinction between the different castes. The sum total of such beliefs, traditions and convictions constitutes the social myth that made the caste system possible.

Social myths are collections of popular beliefs and perceptions that underpin the structure of a society. The acceptance of male dominance in agricultural communities was justified and reinforced by a variety of social myths. The social myth of male superiority that has held Christianity in its grip originated in Hellenistic and Roman societies.

In ancient Greco-Roman culture, women were

considered inferior to men by nature. People who lived in that culture were totally ignorant of the contribution of the female ovum in procreation. They thought men were perfect human beings because they produce "seed" (*semen*), that is, the substance that carries future human beings. Some humans are born as women through a mistake at birth. Women are therefore born incomplete. An essential part is missing. They are "defective." Women retain their usefulness, however: When man has cast his seed into their womb, they feed the child as a field feeds a crop. But women are intellectually and bodily substandard, according to this myth.

The influential philosopher Aristotle (384-322 B.C.) held some mistaken, even shocking, notions about female inferiority. He wrote:

"A male is male in virtue of a particular ability, and a female in virtue of a particular inability.

"A woman is, as it were, an infertile male – she is inferior by nature.

"It is the best for all tame animals to be ruled by human beings. For this is how they are kept alive. In the same way, the relationship between the male and the female is *by nature* such that the male is higher, the female lower, that the male rules and the female is ruled."

Not surprisingly, this kind of thinking was reflected in women's low social status. According to Roman family law, the husband was the wife's absolute lord and master. The wife was the property of her husband and completely subject to his disposition. He could punish her in any way he liked. As far as family property was concerned, the wife herself did not own anything. Everything she or her children inherited belonged to her husband, including the dowry which she brought with her to her marriage.

In civil law, too, women's rights were very limited. The reasons given in Roman law for restraining women's rights are variously described as *"the weakness of her sex"* or *"the stupidity of her sex."* The context makes clear that the problem did not lie in women's physical weakness, but in what was perceived as her lack of sound judgment and her inability to think logically. The results were disastrous. Women could not hold any public office. Women could not act in their own person in court cases, make contracts, testify as witnesses, and so on. Women were, in fact, grouped with minors, slaves, convicted criminals and persons who were dumb and mute; that is, with people whose judgment could not be trusted. In spite of a slight relaxation in laws which offered more protection to women in the Roman Empire of the third and fourth centuries, the overall *inferior status* of women remained the same.

In the West, cultural prejudice against women

forced women into inequality in practically every sphere of life: education, jobs, sports, political maturity and leadership, the sciences, and family life. It is only in our own days that we have seen women rightly slowly regain their innate equality as human beings and citizens.

And the process of liberation is by no means complete. Prejudice still clouds the sky in organised religion.

* * * * *

For nearly 20 centuries, Christianity, too, has been in the grip of the social myth of women's intellectual, moral, private and public inferiority. This myth has obscured the thinking of church fathers, popes, ecclesiastical synods, medieval theologians, you name it.

The presumed inferiority of women entered Church Law especially through the *Decretum Gratiani* (1140 A.D.) – which became official Church Law in 1234 A.D. This was a vital part of the *Corpus Iuris Canonici* that was in force until 1916. The Law was based on writings of Church fathers, local synods, popes and bishops. It laid down the official position held by the Church. Here are excerpts from the Law:

• "Woman" signifies "weakness of mind."

• In everything, a wife is subject to her husband because of her state of servitude.

• Woman is not created in the image of God.

- Wives are subject to their husbands by nature.
- Women may not be given a liturgical office in the church.
- Women cannot become priests or deacons.

Notice, none of these laws are justified by reference to Jesus. Women were deemed inadequate simply because of their inferior status. This universal Church Law determined not only how dioceses, parishes and church tribunals were run, but also what was expected in people's personal and family lives.

Warped views of women held
by Thomas Aquinas and Bonaventure

St. Thomas Aquinas (1225-1274) has always been held out by popes as a great Doctor of the Church, champion of Catholic theology, a touchstone of orthodoxy. Well, Thomas follows Aristotle in considering each woman a mishap at birth, a failed male. He wrote:

> A female is deficient and unintentionally caused. For the active power of the semen always seeks to produce a thing completely like itself, something male. So if a female is produced, this must be because the semen is weak or because the material [provided by the female parent] is unsuitable, or because of the action of some external factor such as the winds from the south which make the atmosphere humid ....
>
> If it were not for some [divine] power that wanted the feminine sex to exist, the birth of a

woman would be just another accident....

Women are still useful, of course. In God's overall scheme they serve the purpose of being the fertile fields in which men can sow their seed, as Aristotle had already pointed out.

Thomas Aquinas offers other observations based on myth as well: Yes, men are intellectually superior to women, for men have a greater power of reason since God equipped them for intellectual tasks. Women not so. Men were created fully in God's image; like God, they are made to rule, to take charge of things. Women are not. They reflect God's image only indirectly, that is, in as far as having a mind they resemble men. For all these reasons, women are naturally subject to men.

And now you understand, Thomas says, why women cannot be priests: because of their inferiority, because they do not measure up to Christ, who as a man was a perfect human being. He further asserts:

> The male sex is required for receiving (Holy) Orders. It is required for the validity of the sacrament ... for since a sacrament is a sign, signifying the object is required in all sacramental actions.... Accordingly, since it is not possible in the female sex to signify eminence of degree, for a woman is in the state of subjection, it follows that she cannot receive the sacrament of Orders....

And here the cat is out of the bag.

Thomas Aquinas, the pinnacle of reliable

Catholic theology, proclaims women are excluded from ordination, not on account of some command by Jesus, but because of their inferiority. It has always been so. Throughout the 20 centuries of its history the institutional Church has excluded women from the priesthood because of their presumed inferior status.

In my own publication, *The Ordination of Women in the Catholic Church*, I have fully documented the evidence for this and provided an ample bibliography. Women's inequality in religious matters was caused by *cultural prejudice* no less than their inequality at the ballot box was, or in employment, in college studies, in academic posts, or whatever.

Of course, over the course of time Church leaders have occasionally blamed Jesus for the exclusion of women. So did medieval theologians Richard of Middleton, John Duns Scotus and Durandus of Saint Pourçain, for instance. But St. Bonaventure (1217-74), like Thomas Aquinas, does not mention a command by Jesus. Instead he, too, simply asserts women's inferior status:

> In Holy Orders spiritual power is given to the ordained; but a woman is not capable of such power.... It must be said that this [the exclusion of women] comes not so much from the institution of the Church as from this fact, that the sacrament of Orders is not suitable for women. For in this sacrament the person who is ordained signifies

Christ the Mediator, and since the Mediator was only of the male sex, he can [only] be signified by the male sex. Therefore the capability of receiving Orders is suitable only to men, who alone can naturally represent him, and by the reception of the character [of Holy Orders] in fact bear his sign.

The vast majority of scholars who study such matters, including Catholics, acknowledge cultural prejudice to be the cause of women's exclusion from ordained ministries. Because of the Vatican's suppression of free speech in Catholic institutions, many academics have fallen silent on this subject in recent decades.

But behind the façade, the academic world fully realises: Excluding women from ordination is simply surrendering to the ancient social myth.

Chapter 4

Don't blame it on Jesus!

By choosing men to form the Twelve, Jesus did not
lay down a permanent norm. He never intended
to exclude women from the priesthood.

Rome claims that if Jesus had wanted to, he
could have chosen women to be part of his
team of Apostles.

"In calling only men as his Apostles, Christ acted
in a completely free and sovereign manner," Rome
says.

This assumption is then interpreted as Jesus
establishing an immutable rule: Only men have a
place in his priesthood.

In reality, Jesus was very much hampered by the
"social myth" of the world in which he lived. Choosing men as leaders was the natural thing for him to
do. Moreover, since the twelve he appointed would

represent the New Israel to replace the twelve patriarchs of the past, it made sense to appoint men. But in no way was the composition of his team set as a permanent rule.

I remember how, years ago, I had a running argument with a teenage student about Jesus as a chess player.

"Chess did not exist in Jesus' time," I said. "And if it did exist, he would have to work out each move one at a time just as any other chess player."

"Nonsense!" the student replied. "Jesus knew everything. He would know every single move of his opponent long before the man himself had worked it out."

Not true, of course.

Christian faith teaches us that Jesus is not only truly God but also truly human. As a person of his time, Jesus was limited in what he knew. Of course, Jesus' sharp spiritual perception heightened by mystical encounters with his Father made him aware of realities others could not see. Like Nathaniel's prayer sessions and the marital mess of the Samaritan woman. Like his foreseeing his passion and resurrection. But he didn't know of all the scientific discoveries that are now common knowledge. He did not know the earth is round. Nor had he ever heard of the "Big Bang," of galaxies, of the moons circling round Jupiter. Evolution, nuclear physics nor global warming would have made sense to him.

In the same way, Jesus did not realise all the social implications of human rights. Yes, he preached that God is love and that all people are God's children and should experience God's love. But the full *social* consequences of this principle lay beyond his grasp. He never thought of trade unions, industrial tribunals, legislation by parliament. He did not campaign for the abolition of slavery or education for all. True, history proves that Christian principles would play a key role in bringing about the full recognition of what we call human rights, but Jesus himself had to live with the immediate social realities of his day.

Choosing twelve male apostles was the natural thing for Jesus to do

Before Jesus surrounded himself with a team of close assistants, he decided on the number twelve. This was no random number. Its significance was clear to any Jew at the time. The twelve apostles would represent the new Israel, to replace the twelve patriarchs of old. For effective symbolism, the twelve had to be men.

Moreover, in Jewish society it was the men who exercised authority. They held the leadership roles. Jesus accepted this reality.

For the Jews, the man was the undisputed head of the family. All relationships centered around him. It was the father who had absolute authority over his children and could decide about their future. Family property was inherited by men, not by women; only if no male heir was left could a daughter inherit. It was the father who, as sole owner of the family property, could distribute it to his sons. Jesus' teaching presupposes these realities.

In the parable of the Prodigal Son, it is the father who distributes the property among his sons. The willing son and the unwilling one are given their work by their father. In all his parables Jesus conforms to the Jewish idea according to which the man was the center of the family. The "owner of the house" is always a man. It is the man who builds the house and defends it against intruders.

When speaking about marriage, Jesus takes the man-centered concept of the Jews for granted. He speaks of a king arranging a marriage for his son, without ever mentioning the queen. At the wedding itself, it is not the bride but the bridegroom who is celebrated. The wedding guests are called "the friends of the bridegroom."

Is it not abundantly clear from all this that Jesus accepted the reality of the pre-eminent position accorded to men in his own time?

All leaders in society at the time – whether governors, generals or priests – were men. If this was the cultural climate of the day, need we be surprised that Jesus called only men to be his apostles? To put it differently: entrusting leadership to women would have required a profound social revolution.

Even if Jesus had wanted to overthrow the social structures of his society, it is doubtful that he could have achieved this in so short a time. A centuries-old social myth that is ingrained in the texture of people's lives couldn't be uprooted in the course of Jesus's three-year public ministry.

And Jesus did not effect immediate social liberations. Although his teaching and redemptive action enshrined the principles that would make true social equality possible, Jesus himself refrained from any direct social rebellion. Although his attitude toward women shows that he recognised their value and their potential, he did not campaign for women's emancipation.

He was here for a different purpose.

In selecting only men for membership on his team of apostles, Jesus simply followed the prevailing social limitations imposed on all by contemporary society. And, as symbols of the New Israel replacing the old twelve patriarchs, choosing twelve men was the logical thing to do.

Jesus did not establish a permanent norm that excludes women forever

It is abundantly clear from all the evidence we have that Jesus's selection of the all-male Twelve did not rule out female spiritual leadership in the future. Let's look at the facts.

To begin with, Jesus never explicitly stated he wanted only men to be apostles, or that he did not want women. The absence of a woman among the original twelve is a purely *negative fact.* Negative facts prove nothing – as other Gospel texts illustrate. Consider the following two examples.

• Jesus ordered his apostles to travel as the poor did. His orders were even stricter than that: They should walk as the poorest of the poor – barefoot. "Take no gold, nor silver, nor copper coins in your belt, no bag for your journey, nor two tunics, nor sandals, nor a staff!" Jesus rode on a donkey at times, but did not ride on horseback. Jesus did not – repeat, did not – mention the modern modes of travel like cars, buses and airplanes. He did not mention suitcases, wallets and travellers' cheques. How can bishops and priests today presume to use such modern modes and tools of travel?

• At the Last Supper, while instituting the Eucharistic meal, Jesus clearly stated: "Take and eat, all of you!" Jesus did not – repeat, did not – say that the Eucharistic bread could be preserved to take communion to the sick; and certainly not that it could be kept in a tabernacle for days on end. How could the Church presume to adopt such practices?

Examples like these can be multiplied. If the negative norm of Jesus *not* having said or done something is taken to imply a permanent decision, many legitimate later decisions by the Church therefore would be totally invalid. In the same way, stating that the omission of women from the original

Twelve constitutes a permanent norm makes no sense.

Hang on, Rome says. *The permanent norm of omitting women can be proved from Tradition, from the fact that the Church has never ordained women.*

Well, as we have seen in the previous chapter, that is not true. The constant rejection of women in earlier centuries is not justified in Tradition by referring to Jesus, except sporadically. This tradition was openly based on women's presumed inferiority; it was due to the overwhelming cultural prejudice against women.

Finally, we know from the study of Church history that the institution of the Twelve was only a temporary measure. Its features were soon abandoned. The original apostles were all Jews, but the "overseers" *(episkopoi)* who took over leadership were selected from many nations. The apostles received power to drive out unclean spirits and cure the sick. This new authority of the apostles was a distinguishing mark of their ministry. They were specifically sent out to drive out demons and cure sick people so that their preaching would be more easily believed. Although the Acts of the Apostles still mention such miracles being performed by Peter and Paul, the driving out of demons and curing of the sick were not maintained as a standard part of the priestly ministry.

In fact, the Twelve as a team of core leaders soon

disappeared from the scene. After Jesus' death, the apostles were reduced to eleven because of Judas' defection and suicide. The apostles took pains to appoint a successor to fill up the number. But soon after that, as new leaders were needed in many early church communities, the number twelve itself was abandoned.

The Twelve had known Jesus personally and had witnessed his passion and resurrection. This team of Aramaic-speaking, all-Jewish Palestinians enjoyed a significant function in the Early Church – but it was only temporary.

Why would the fact that they all happened to be men have constituted a permanent norm for the later priesthood? And why does the Church continue to cling to this mistaken notion?

Chapter 5

Jesus' positive attitude toward women

We know from Jesus' words and actions that he would have been open to future developments in his Church – including women's greater participation in the ministry.

Matthew, Mark, Luke and John – the four Evangelists – not only reported on Jesus' time on Earth but they interpreted the meaning of many of the events of his life. They went beyond giving just a plain record of historical facts.

In doing so – and writing under inspiration – they added valuable layers of understanding and showed surprising new possibilities, particularly in the Gospel of Luke.

Luke's Gospel is of special interest as far as women are concerned. Luke points to Jesus' awareness of women's basic equality and unrealised potential. Although Jesus refrained from being a social reformer in this as in other fields, Luke teaches us that many of Jesus' words and actions seem to imply that he would be open to women's greater participation in the ministry in the future.

Luke presented Jesus' message to Greek-speaking non-Jews, who were known as Hellenists. He wrote for converts in the Middle East who were influenced by Greek culture. History shows that Hellenistic women enjoyed much more freedom and played a more active role in society than their Jewish or Roman counterparts.

Hellenistic culture in Asia Minor was much more open to women. Women could become leaders. Women could hold leadership positions such as being business owners, administrators of property, and local magistrates. Luke goes out of his way to show that Jesus' attitude should be encouraging to women.

To do justice to Scripture, we sometimes have to go beyond a narrow interpretation of the text. We often need to approach the Gospel in a more reflective way, as Luke does. To truly understand the Scriptures – the inspired Word – we should aim at penetrating into its core, listening attentively to what it says by implication as well as by express statement, and capturing intuitively the deeper insights of the message. For then we discover fascinating *pointers.*

First, we need to realize some key elements of Luke's theology. What was important to him?

• Luke is concerned about the exaggerated expectations of his contemporaries regarding the Last Day. He teaches that before Christ's coming we should recognise *the period of the Church.*

• Luke points out that we can expect new developments during this *period of the Church.* These new developments, though not explicitly contained in Jesus' message, do have a divine origin. They derive from the action of the Holy Spirit within the Church.

• Luke shows us that many of these new developments are implicitly contained in what Jesus said or did. When writing his Gospel, Luke sees in many events of Jesus' life *a vision of things to come.*

• Luke makes it clear that it was natural for the Early Church to develop new ministries. The focus on women in Luke's Gospel points to possibilities of their future participation in the ministry.

This may seem like a rather long path to travel, but it is well worth the trouble. Luke teaches that we should expect new developments in the Church, including changes in the ministry. It seems that, under inspiration, Luke is speaking precisely about the question that is now before us: Can there be in the Church a new participation of women in the ministry — though not explicitly foreseen in the

Gospel?

Luke's answer would be a resounding "Yes."

The 'era of the Church'
and the Acts of the Apostles

After the resurrection of Jesus it took the apostolic community quite some time to realise that a new era had begun: *the era of the Church.*

Many among the earlier Christians were convinced that the second coming of Jesus would occur very soon. Jesus' cryptic saying – "Some of those standing here will not taste death before they have seen the Kingdom of God come in power" – was interpreted to mean that the end of the world would come within a few years. From what Paul wrote to the Thessalonians in 51 A.D., we know that he expected that he himself and most of his fellow Christians would be alive when Christ was to come.

But before the end of time would come, Christ wanted there to be an *era of the Church.* Luke thought this so important that he devoted a whole book to it, the *Acts of the Apostles.* For Luke, it was a fundamental mistake to identify Christianity solely with the life of Jesus because, as Luke realised, God was continuing to act through the Spirit after Jesus' redemptive work. The Acts of the Apostles have rightly been called the Gospel of the Holy Spirit. For, starting from Jesus' promise of the Spirit in the first chapter and the account of Pentecost in the second, Luke shows throughout the Acts how the Holy Spirit made Jesus' followers into a world Church.

By recognising the independent role of the Church, Luke drew attention to a theological fact of paramount importance: Jesus himself had not decided about everything that should be done in his Church.

New and unexpected developments would take place among Jesus' followers. These new developments, too, have a divine origin. They are brought about by the Holy Spirit from within the Church. They should be accepted with equal readiness as the explicit rulings of Jesus himself. Of course, there is no contradiction between what Jesus said and did and the new directives given by the Spirit.

When writing his Gospel, Luke shows that Jesus' words and actions contained a deeper dimension, a "vision" that would find expression in such far-reaching decisions to be made later by the Church.

For example, Luke narrates in the Acts of the Apostles how the Early Church came to accept non-Jews into their community. The baptism of the household of Cornelius was truly a new beginning here. Previously, non-Jews had been admitted only if they were Jewish converts who had been circumcised. Cornelius and his household were Romans who became Christians without first being made imitation-Jews by circumcision.

When Peter preached the Gospel of Jesus, Cornelius and his family were filled with the Holy Spirit. It was most of all this clear manifestation of the Holy Spirit that convinced Peter that pagans can become Christians without an intermediate stage of circumcision.

Admitting non-Jews without requiring circumcision was a momentous decision that was not made by Jesus but by the Church. It went far beyond what Jesus said.

A second example: We know from the Gospels that Jesus restricted his own ministry explicitly to the Jews.

"Do not take the road to gentile lands, and do not enter any Samaritan town. But go rather to the lost sheep of the house of Israel," Jesus said. "I was sent to the lost sheep of the house of Israel, and to them alone."

It was necessary for the Early Christians to become somewhat detached from a too-literal adherence to Jesus' words. They had to learn that in order to understand Jesus' mind we should not limit ourselves to his external sayings and deeds alone. We should grasp above all the prophetic dimension in Jesus' life – which went far beyond his immediate practice.

If we read the Gospel of St. Luke in this light, we see how he handles this inner vision and prophetic dimension. Luke reflects on Jesus' attitude towards Samaritans, people considered heretics and religious outcasts by the Jews. Jesus refused to curse the Samaritan village that failed to give him accommodation. He said about the centurion at Capernaum, "I tell you, nowhere, even in Israel, have I found faith like this."

In incidents such as these Luke rightly sees an attitude of Jesus towards non-Jews that transcends Mosaic law and that embraces a vision of the Church in which Samaritans and Romans can feel at home as much as the Jews.

New ministry and 'apostolic succession'

Pointing to new forms of ministry is another of Luke's explicit aims. There is evidence to show that the question of "apostolic succession" was not so easily solved in the early Church. The twelve apostles who had been chosen by Christ himself and who had been personally instructed by him were accorded such an exceptional respect and authority that it looked as if no one else could take their places.

Yet succession was essential for the continued existence and spread of the Church. However privileged a position the Twelve occupied, their task had to be continued by persons who had not been directly chosen by Christ himself.

When writing the Acts of the Apostles, Luke tackles this problem head on. In the very first chapter he narrates how Matthias was chosen to replace Judas. Complaints from the Greek-speaking Christians at Jerusalem that they were being neglected led to the appointment of seven deacons. Although the original purpose of this diaconate focused more on material ministration, it is clear from the accounts of two of them – Stephen and Philip – that they were doing the same work as the apostles as far as preaching the Gospel is concerned. But they could not bring the Holy Spirit by the imposition of hands.

A complete breakthrough took place at Antioch when the congregation there, under the guidance of the Holy Spirit, laid their hands on Paul and Barnabas and sent them on a missionary tour. Their official status was confirmed in the Council of Jerusalem. This opened the way to many others being drawn into the ministry, such as Timothy from Lystra, Titus from Galatia, and Apollos from Alexandria.

In keeping with his ability to see a future vision in Jesus' actions, Luke searched the life of Jesus to find confirmation for this development in the Church. He found it in the fact that Jesus sent out more disciples than only the Twelve. In his Gospel, Luke makes much of this event. After reporting how Jesus sent out the Twelve, he recounts how Jesus sent out 72 others who were given the same instructions as the apostles. Just as twelve stands for the twelve tribes of Israel, so 72 denotes all the nations of the earth, according to the Jewish symbolism of the time.

For St. Luke, this missioning of the 72 had prophetic value as it pointed to what needed to happen in the later Church.

Chapter 6

Women in the Gospel of Luke

Women were closely associated with Jesus on his apostolic tours. To Luke's way of thinking, this points to the possibility of their expanded roles during 'the era of the Church.'

All four Gospels affirm that women played a special part in Jesus' life, but none more so than the writings of St. Luke.

Luke records episodes not found in the other Gospel accounts. He introduces Elizabeth, the prophetess Anna, the widow of Naim, the women who ministered unto Jesus, the woman who was bent over, and the weeping women of Jerusalem.

Luke preserved two special parables involving women: the housewife who lost her coin and the tenacious widow. Women also mentioned in the other Gospels receive special attention from Luke: Mary Magdalene, Mary and Martha, and the poor widow who offered two coins in the temple.

Why did Luke focus so much attention on the role played by women in Jesus' life? Obviously, here, as in the other cases, Luke acted in response to a need in the Early Church.

In many communities women played important roles. In Corinth it was Chloë who sent messengers to Paul to inform him about problems in the Church. The community of Cenchreae had a lady deacon, "Phoebe, our fellow-Christian." At Philippi, where Luke worked a long time in the apostolate, we find mention of three prominent ladies: Lydia, who ran a prosperous business in purple dresses and in whose house the local community met; and Euodia and Syntyche, about whom Paul said "these women who shared my struggles in the cause of the Gospel."

When recalling incidents of Jesus' life involving women, Luke has a rich message to give. In his view, women are equal recipients of Jesus' grace. Like men, women too should be converted (Mary Magdalene), listen to Jesus' words (Mary and Martha), pray with perseverance (the tenacious widow), and share in his sufferings and cross. The role of being a mother, with its sorrows and joys, is reflected in persons such as the widow of Naim, Elizabeth, and Our Lady.

Jesus takes examples from women's everyday tasks: drawing water from the well, grinding corn with the millstones, sweeping the house, mixing leaven through the dough, and preparing food for guests. Jesus had observed such activities and vested some of them with profound symbolic meaning. In these and many other ways Luke's passages that involve women yield a rich treasury of pointers and reflections.

A future ministry of women

Did St. Luke allude to the ministry of women?

Did he, in presenting these words and deeds of Jesus, want to call attention to women's involvement in the apostolate?

Does St. Luke's Gospel contain a "vision" of how women could be given a broader role within the Christian community?

It is in the light of these questions that certain passages in Luke's Gospel take on a profound significance. Luke relates how women, too, accompanied Jesus in his apostolic mission:

> Jesus went journeying from town to town and village to village, proclaiming the good news of the Kingdom of God. With him were the Twelve and a number of women who had been set free from evil spirits and infirmities: Mary, known as Mary of Magdala, from whom seven devils had come out; Joanna, the wife of Chusa, a steward of Herod's; Susanna; and many others. These women provided for them out of their own

resources.

Luke realised that, given the social status of women in those days, it was impossible for Jesus to draw them into the apostolic team. In the early Church as Luke knew it, a truly equal partnership of women in the ministry was also excluded – on sociological grounds.

But it is certain that Luke, who is the only evangelist to recount this aspect of Jesus' ministry, records the above incident because he saw it had prophetic value. If women were so closely associated with Jesus on his apostolic tours, this would certainly imply for Luke the possibility of a much greater participation of women in the future – in *the era of the Church.*

And what about Anna, the prophetess?

Again, Luke is the only evangelist to make mention of her. According to his description, she lived alone as a widow "to the age of eighty-four." She is a person totally dedicated to God: "She never left the temple, but worshipped day and night, fasting and praying." Having met Jesus, she became a witness to him.

"She talked about the child to all who were looking for the liberation of Jerusalem," Luke notes in his Gospel.

Why did Luke present this picture of Anna, the mature and dedicated woman, the prophetess who preached about Jesus? Once more, was it not because in her he saw a vision of things to come? In the witness of this woman, Luke foresaw an apostolic task meant for women that could not be realised as yet in his own times.

But isn't this what inspiration is about? Wasn't this exactly Luke's constant preoccupation, namely, to show that not all decisions had been made in Jesus' life, that completely new developments were possible under the guidance of the Holy Spirit?

Our Lady's role in Luke's Gospel

At the same time Mary heard of her election to be the mother of the Son of God, she also received a commission. She was told by Gabriel that Elizabeth had conceived. Mary set out on her mission. Entering Zechariah's house, she greeted Elizabeth.

"When Elizabeth heard Mary's greeting, the baby stirred in her womb. Then Elizabeth was filled with the Holy Spirit," Luke writes.

It was Mary's mediation, her coming, her voice, her person that brought this grace of the Holy Spirit.

Traditional Catholic belief has rightly dwelt on the exalted position of Mary as the Mother of Christ. It has stressed Mary's role in redemption, her share in the dispensation of grace. Has it thereby not acknowledged in Mary the heart of the priestly function?

Vatican II states:

She conceived, brought forth and nourished Christ. She presented him to the Father in the Temple. She shared her Son's sufferings as he died on the cross. Thus, in a wholly singular way she co-operated by her obedience, faith, hope and burning charity in the work of the Saviour in restoring supernatural life to souls. For this reason she is a mother to us in the order of grace.

Was there ever a priest so near to Christ's sacrifice as Mary was? And as to her prophetic role:

The Mother of God joyfully showed her firstborn son to the shepherds and the Magi.... At the marriage feast of Cana, moved with pity, she brought about by her intercession the beginning of the miracles of Jesus as Messiah....

In fact, through her charismatic intercession at Cana, Mary mediates in bringing about a Eucharistic symbol: the changing of water into wine.

We all know that Our Lady did not in fact exercise the priestly functions that the apostles did. As far as we know, she did not preside at the Eucharistic table to break the bread. She did not travel round to preach, baptise and impose hands. In the social climate of those times, such functions were performed by men only, not by women. As Christ accepted this social fact, so did Mary.

But is it not all the more remarkable that the evangelists, and especially Luke, dwell on Mary's prominent role and praise her more than any person except Christ himself? Did Luke, with his vision of new things to come in the Church, not deliberately draw attention to Mary to give courage to women?

It seems theologically sound to say that Mary's personality and her role in redemption established once and for all the complete equality of women in God's eyes and, therefore, by right, in the Church. This would naturally include the capability of acting in the name of Christ at the Eucharist table or in the confessional.

Mary of Magdala

It is common knowledge from the Gospels that Mary of Magdala accompanied Jesus on many of his apostolic tours. Luke further narrates about her that she, with other disciples, watched the crucifixion of Jesus, helped at his burial, and was among the first to learn about the resurrection on Easter morning.

However, for the same cultural and sociological reasons explained earlier, Mary of Magdala could not have taken up the position of an Apostle of Christ. I believe that, especially in St. Luke's Gospel, we have here a vision of the possibilities that go much beyond the social limitations of the time.

Recall the episode of the sinful woman who weeps at Jesus' feet as he reclines in a Pharisee's house. This woman may have been Mary of

Magdala; in Luke's eyes, she certainly was the same kind of person. Jesus says about her:

> You see this woman? I came to your house: you provided no water for my feet; but this woman has made my feet wet with her tears and wiped them with her hair. You gave me no kiss; but she has been kissing my feet ever since I came in. You did not anoint my head with oil; but she has anointed my feet with myrrh.

It is as if Jesus is speaking to us across the centuries: *What is all this discussion,* he might say, *about women in the ministry? What makes you think I would turn them away from the sanctuary or from my altar? Have I not always stressed the real thing rather than accidentals?*

When I was in the house of Simon the Pharisee, did I not praise the sinful woman for exercising the ministry of the footwashing? It was not her status, nor her previous sins, but her love that counted in my eyes.

By her kiss of welcome, by washing my feet, by her gift of ointment, it was she who was my minister at that moment more than all the men who sat around.

Would I refuse any woman to be my minister who could serve my Body, the Church, in the same way: by breaking the bread, by pouring the water of baptism or anointing the sick?

Don't you think I am happy that women in your time are at last given that position in society that is rightly theirs? Would I not recognise the real contribution a woman priest can make in the new world you are living in now?

Jesus' understanding of and respect for women like Mary of Magdala is an unmistakable "pointer" that reveals his true mind.

Conclusion

While some of my thoughts in this chapter may have gone beyond the limits of rigid scriptural argumentation, my reflections are based on Scripture and I believe I have captured something of value that is liable to be lost in logical debate. God sometimes says more in Scripture by suggestions, hints and pointers than by flat statements. Scripture, too, has its dimension of *vision* and is unavoidably vague as it deals with the future.

Luke helps us open our eyes. Jesus' respect for women, his appreciation of their potential and their role in his mission point to their potentially unlimited scope in the future.

But is there more? Did Jesus in fact make decisions that amounted to an implicit acceptance of women's full participation in the ministry?

Chapter 7

Christ's new priesthood

Christ the Lord instituted a new priesthood,
open to women, too, through baptism and love.

It may be surprising to learn that Christ's
"priesthood" is not based on sacred entities,
but rather is rooted in the realities of our everyday
world. And it might come as a bit of a shock to
hear that a Christian priest is no "sacred person,"
but instead is defined as someone who ministers
Christ's saving presence to others in ordinary ways.

The early Christian communities in, say, Athens
celebrated the Eucharist not in church but in their
family homes. The presiding "elder" (*presbyter*)
would wear his or her daily tunic. People would
gather around a wooden table and share the
consecrated bread and wine from ordinary vessels.

Yet Christ was not less present among them than

in a medieval cathedral. Perhaps he was even more tangibly present as the spiritual reality transforming our everyday world. For Christ replaced a priesthood based on sacrality – that is, the quality of being holy, or sacred – by a priesthood based on grace.

A priesthood without 'sacred' realities

During the first three centuries, Christian communities fully lived Christ's sacramental presence within everyday life. But as the Church became more accepted in society, it began to assume the sacrality ideas of Old Testament times and the pagan Roman empire. Places for worship became "hallowed" churches, the cup became a chalice, the priest's garment a sacred chasuble, and so on. And the priest, too, was no longer an elder (*presbyter*) but a "holy man" (*sacerdos*).

The Vatican Congregation for Divine Worship still promotes the ideology of sacrality. The Eucharist takes place in the sanctuary: a *sacred* area within the church in which the altar stands and in which consecrated ministers exercise their offices. The altar itself is a *sacred* table and should be treated as such. The ambo, from which the Scripture is read, is a *sacred* lectern. The chalice and the paten that hold the consecrated bread and wine are called *sacred* vessels. The priest wears *sacred* vestments and is himself a *consecrated* person.

Even the chair on which the priest sits in the sanctuary shares in his *sacredness*. It has to be "visibly distinguished from chairs used by others who are not clergy." The chalice and the paten are to be "clearly distinguished from vessels designed for everyday use." The priest's vestments should stand out from everyday dress. All these sacred objects, including the priest's chair, are blessed through special prayers.

What would Jesus have said about all this?

Jesus was not a social reformer; he didn't take part in any social revolution. The same cannot be said about his involvement in religion.

Though he was tolerant and accommodating regarding the social structures of his time, he was intolerant regarding antiquated and inadequate religious structures. In this field his action could hardly have been more ruthless. He utterly abolished the priesthood as it was understood in Old Testament terms.

To understand the full implications of Jesus' attitude in this matter, we should recall that the Old Testament priesthood rested on a philosophy that distinguished between the sacred and the "profane." Some everyday realities, such as houses, cattle, eating and sleeping, doing business, and so on, were considered ordinary or "profane." It was thought by many that the Divine was not really directly present in these realities. Other realities of our world, however, were considered to have been penetrated with Divine presence and to have become *sacred* on that account.

This is the origin of *sacred* times (the sabbath and feast days), *sacred* places (mainly the temple), *sacred* objects (e.g., vessels used for worship), and *sacred* persons (priests) consecrated to God. The Old Testament priest was separated from other men on the same basis as the sabbath was considered holier than the Monday, or the temple was a more *sacred* place than the marketplace. The priest was the embodiment of a divine presence in a profane world.

But Jesus overthrew this whole system.

He did not just substitute new holy realities for the old ones, he went further. He radically abrogated *the distinction itself* between the sacred and the profane; he did away with it. This may seem startling to some Catholics, including Vatican *monsignori*, who continue to think along Old Testament lines. They imagine the New Testament to be an updated version of the Old. They think our churches have taken the place of the temple at Jerusalem, that our Sunday replaces the sabbath, and that the New Testament priest is a polished version of the Old Testament one.

The cause of this misunderstanding is partly due to developments within the Church in the course of her history, partly in deference towards the human necessity of having quasi-sacred realities like churches as part of an established religion.

But basically the clinging to *sacred* realities is a regression – and is contrary to the teachings of the New Testament.

Take the example of *sacred place*. The Jews were allowed to sacrifice only in the temple, and even within the temple each place became holier the nearer one approached its center. The inner chamber of the sanctuary, called "Holy of Holies," could be entered only by the high priest and then only once a year.

Christ no longer acknowledges such holy places. He sanctified all places. In his kingdom, worship can be given not only in Jerusalem or on a holy mountain, but anywhere so long as it is done "in spirit and in truth," as we have learned in the Gospel of John. In fact, Christ's own body was the new temple that could substitute for the old in any part of the world. When Jesus celebrated the Eucharist for the first time at the Last Supper, he did so in the upper room of an ordinary house. To crown it all, the place he chose for bringing his unique sacrifice for the whole world was not the temple court but an ugly hill of execution.

When Jesus died, the distinction between sacred and profane places was wiped out once and for all. The Gospels record that at the crucifixion the curtain of the temple, which screened off the Holy of Holies, "was torn in two, from top to bottom." The Early Church realised this. They had no temples, churches or chapels. They celebrated common prayer and the Eucharist wherever they gathered as a community. The same has basically remained true of the Church today, even though the custom of setting aside places for prayer has returned.

The same holds good for *sacred days*. For the Jews, the sabbath was a day consecrated to God on which people were not allowed to work for their own profit. Jesus frequently clashed with the Pharisees because he refused to suspend his apostolate on the sabbath. Conflicts arose when, on the sabbath, his disciples plucked ears of corn, when Jesus cured a man with a withered hand in the synagogue, when he healed a man who had dropsy, and when he gave sight to the blind man at Siloam.

Jesus' most revolutionary statement in the discussion was: "The sabbath was made for human beings, not human beings for the sabbath." In other words, the sabbath does not derive its value from itself, from being *sacred time* of some kind or other, but from serving a human need.

Whereas the Old Testament priests had to offer frequently at specified *sacral times*, Jesus sanctified the totality of time by his all-sufficient sacrifice. With Jesus' death, the sabbath and all these sacral times had become meaningless. From now on, any day and any hour of the day could be the appropriate time for prayer and celebration.

The Christian practice of celebrating the Eucharist on the first day of the week because Christ rose on that day led to the practice of weekly Mass on Sundays. However, the Sunday was not a new sabbath for the Early Christians.

Having seen Jesus's attitude towards sacred time and place, we will not be surprised to see his same attitude towards *sacred priesthood*. He put an end to the priesthood as defined in Old Testament times. He distanced himself from any priesthood understood as a sacral institution and established a new priesthood built on "the power of indestructible life."

The Old Testament notions of the priesthood were alien to Jesus; we never find him applying the term "priest" to himself or his followers. In fact, it is only in the letter to the Hebrews that the "priesthood" of Christ is mentioned in explicit terms and compared with the priesthood of the Old Testament (See Heb 5, 1-4; 7, 26-28).

Jesus entrusted a special task to his apostles and their successors, but he would not have agreed to this ministry being understood as setting apart a new sacred group as had been the case in Old Testament times. The later developments in the Church which favoured such a separation would certainly have alarmed and saddened him.

Now, all this discussion about Jesus distancing himself from sacred things and places may seem negative, even destructive. But actually the opposite is true: In doing so, Jesus re-affirmed the sacredness of the whole "profane" world. And was this not also Francis of Assisi's joyful discovery as he sang the praises of Brother Sun, Sister Moon and Mother Earth, celebrating all the wonders of God's creation, in his *Canticle of the Creatures?* The mystic Pierre Teilhard de Chardin, S.J., expressed it eloquently:

"Lord, help me to see the world with the same beauty it had when it tumbled from your creative hand. Help me to see that nothing here below is profane; on the contrary, everything is sacred."

A priesthood shared by women as well

Christ exercised his priesthood by offering himself on Calvary and by preaching. To continue these two ministries, every disciple has to carry his or her own cross; each of his followers has to bear witness to him even unto persecution and death.

All Christians therefore participate in the royal priesthood of Christ. All can be called "priests to his God and Father" and "priests of God and of Christ." All together they constitute "a kingdom and priesthood to our God."

This common priesthood is given through the Sacrament of Baptism. We should note that this baptism is exactly the same for every single person. There is absolutely no difference in the baptism conferred on women. And this is revolutionary.

In Old Testament times, boys were circumcised on the eighth day after birth. This was an essential condition for belonging to the covenant, more or less parallel to Christian baptism being a condition for belonging to the Church. However, the old dispensation knew no equivalent rite of initiation for women. All this was tantamount to meaning that God had concluded his covenant with the men, the "sons of Israel." The women participated in the covenant only indirectly, through their fathers and husbands. But not so in baptism.

Paul affirms in Galatians 3 that the baptism of Christ transcends and obliterates whatever social differences exist among humankind:

> It is through faith that all of you are God's children in union with Christ Jesus. For all who are baptised into the union of Christ have taken upon themselves the qualities of Christ himself. So there is no difference between Jews and Gentiles, between slaves and free men, between men and women.... You are all one in union with Christ Jesus.

The ordination to the sacramental priesthood is an extension of the basic sacrificial and prophetic sharing that has already been given in baptism. Although the ministerial priesthood adds a new function to the powers received in baptism, it is at the same time intrinsically related to it. Indeed, the Dogmatic Constitution on the Church and Vatican II make it clear:

"Though they differ essentially and not only in degree, the common priesthood of the faithful and the ministerial or hierarchical priesthood are none the less ordered one to the other; each in its own way shares in the one priesthood of Christ."

When the Second Vatican Council says that the sharing in Christ's priesthood through the sacrament of Holy Orders is *essentially* different, it means that baptism by itself does not confer the commission to teach, rule and offer sacrifice in the name of Christ. It does not mean to say that for Holy Orders a different set of discriminating values would hold good. Whatever may be required for ordination to the ministry, it cannot be a *sacred* reality that would make one person intrinsically superior to another. Vatican II is explicit on this:

"There is a common dignity of members deriving from their rebirth in Christ, a common grace as children, a common vocation to perfection, one salvation, one hope and undivided charity. In Christ and in the Church there is, then, no inequality arising from race or nationality, social condition or sex.... Although by Christ's will some are established as teachers, dispensers of the mysteries, and pastors for the others, there remains, nevertheless, a true equality between all with regard to the dignity and the activity that is common to all the faithful in the building up of the Body of Christ."

But if gender cannot be a limiting factor as a

sacred reality, how could it play a role on the level of the sacramental sign?

A priesthood in which charitable service is the sign

We have seen in an earlier chapter that Rome contends Christ's priests have to be male in order to represent Christ, who was a man.

" 'Sacramental signs,' says St. Thomas Aquinas, 'represent what they signify by natural resemblance.' The same natural resemblance is required for persons as for things; when Christ's role in the Eucharist is to be expressed sacramentally, there would not be this natural resemblance which must exist between Christ and his minister if the role of Christ were not taken by a man: in such a case it would be difficult to see in the minister the image of Christ. For Christ himself was and remains a man," according to Pope Paul VI, writing in *Inter Insigniores*.

The claim that Christ is represented better by a man because Christ, too, was a man cannot be substantiated from any scriptural text. The argument given in the Roman document is of a philosophical nature. It is what is known in theology as an "argument based on convenience."

The argument is wrong because the philosophy it presupposes is wrong. The scholastics, to whom the document refers as the source of the argument, put forth a philosophy of the sexes that can no longer be defended by any Christian.

St. Bonaventure (also quoted in the document) maintained that only the male person presents a true image of God. St. Thomas Aquinas concluded that because woman is only an "incomplete man" and thus "cannot signify eminence of degree" that she could not "resemble" Christ or be his "image."

But surely such reasoning contradicts Scripture itself, let alone a better philosophy of human dignity. God's Word links both genders when speaking of divine resemblance: "God created man in the image of himself; in the image of God he created him; male and female he created them."

And St. Paul says that all, men and women, have put on Christ. He speaks of *all* Christians when he says:

> We, with our unveiled faces reflecting like mirrors the brightness of the Lord, all grow brighter and brighter as we are turned into the image that we reflect; this is the work of the Lord, who is Spirit.

* * * * *

By stressing the male gender as such an essential characteristic of the priesthood is the Vatican not under-valuing the priesthood of Christ? What are the features described by Scripture itself as pre-eminent in signifying Christ's presence? If we go by the qualifications seen in Jesus, the high priest, we find the following to be of paramount importance in his priesthood:

- To be called by God (Heb 5, 4)
- Having suffered himself, to be able to help those who are tempted (Heb 2, 18)
- To be able to sympathise with people's weaknesses (Heb 4, 14-16)
- To be able to deal gently with the ignorant and the wayward (Heb 5, 1-10)

This is quite different from requiring that he be a male descendant of Aaron. Jesus's priesthood is indeed a new priesthood ruled by its own laws.

Listening to Jesus himself, we hear him stress *love as the sign he requires*. By laying down his life for his friends Jesus proved his love. It is by such love that the true shepherd is distinguished from the hireling. Readiness to serve, not the power to dominate, makes one to be like Jesus.

Not by presiding at table alone but by washing people's feet is the Master recognised.

One should note that we are not dealing here with a mere moral requirement but with an element that has sign value:

"By this love you have for one another, everyone will know that you are my disciples."

Although Jesus is speaking of love as a commandment, he is here addressing the apostles on the very occasion he is ordaining them as his priests. His "Do this in memory of me" presupposes pastoral love as the special sign by which his priests should be recognised. It is such love that he demands from Peter before entrusting him with the apostolic commission.

Such considerations demonstrate that Scripture itself stresses values such as sympathy, service and love rather than accidentals like being a man.

Would we not be nearer to Christ's mind when we stipulate that a woman filled with the spirit of Christ's pastoral love is a more fitting image of his presence than a man who were to lack such love?

In short, for us Christians, being a priest means being delegated the following:

- To preach Christ's message of love
- To guide people as a good shepherd who cares about each individual
- To support people on their spiritual journey as a servant prepared to wash their feet
- To apply God's forgiveness and healing
- To bring Christ present to the community by saying in his name "This is my body . . . this is my blood."

The definition of Christ's priesthood does not include a requirement of gender.

Judas Iscariot's successor – must have been present to fulfill the requirements stipulated by Peter. Moreover, the two disciples of Emmaus, Cleophas and his companion, were in attendance. They recognised Jesus when he re-enacted the Eucharist in their home following his resurrection, as we know from Luke's Gospel. Cleophas's companion is most likely to have been his wife, Mary; she was one of the disciples who stood under Jesus's cross.

Conclusive proof for women's presence at the Last Supper arises from the fact that it was a Paschal meal.

The Last Supper was a Passover meal

Because the Last Supper was a Passover meal, it would have been attended by both men and women. Scripture scholars recognize numerous parallels between the Last Supper and traditional Jewish Passover meals.

Some scholars have tried to dispute the fact that the Last Supper was a Passover meal; they say it took place a day too early. However, the preponderance of evidence from the Scriptures and other sources clearly shows that it was a Passover meal. For Jesus, it certainly was: "I have longed to eat this Passover with you." (Lk 22, 15)

Though the presence of women at the Last Supper is not mentioned explicitly in the Gospel texts, this means nothing. The same is true for numerous other instances in the Gospels in which women were overlooked or their presence was taken for granted. It was understood that they were in attendance. For instance, in the Gospel of Matthew, we read "those who ate numbered about 5,000 men, not counting the women and children." Again, the women's presence was taken for granted; it went without saying that yes, of course, women were part of the gathering.

By Old Testament law, Passover meals had to be celebrated with the whole family, and often with a neighbour's family, including wives, daughters and grandmothers. So women must have been there. Would Jesus have forgotten his mother at this celebration?

And what about the other female disciples who were undoubtedly in Jerusalem at the time of the Last Supper? The next day they would follow Jesus to Golgotha while the male apostles fled. Jesus would show himself first to women after his resurrection.

It is inconceivable that Jesus would not have invited these women, together with his mother, to join him at his last Passover meal.

Jesus' key words at the institution of the Eucharist are: "Take and eat, this is my body . . . this is the cup of my blood, drink of it *all of you*. Do this in memorial of me." Jesus' words have always, rightly, been interpreted not so much as a request but as a commission: *I empower you to do this to remember me.*

Well, to whom did Jesus address these words?

Matthew says clearly, "He blessed the bread, broke it and gave it to his disciples, saying...." The commission was not given only to the twelve apostles, but to all disciples who were present.

The significance of this was not lost in early tradition. Liturgical texts used at the Eucharist make this clear. The eucharistic canon of the early Roman Rite as found with St. Ambrose refers to both men and women. It reads: Jesus took the bread and "handed it when broken to his apostles *and disciples,*" then took the cup and "handed it to his apostles *and disciples.*" The same formula is still used today by the Coptic and Orthodox Church in the Liturgy of St. Basil and by the Orthodox Church in its regular liturgy of St. John Chrysostom.

Extraordinary ministers of the Eucharist

At the Last Supper, when Jesus instituted the Eucharist he established a fundamental power: *In principle*, he enabled all baptised disciples, including women, to preside at the Eucharist.

The implications of this have not escaped the attention of theologians. Edward Schillebeeckx, for instance, noted that leadership is the "right" of each Christian community. And whoever leads the community is *ipso facto* competent to preside at the Eucharist. While ordination may be the ordinary way to assign someone to leadership, exceptions are possible. It is not dogmatically excluded for some persons in certain circumstances to accede to the ministry. Empowerment to leadership is, in essence, simply "an accentuation and specification" of baptism, Schillebeeckx maintains.

Predictably, Schillebeeckx's view has been denounced by the Congregation for Doctrine. This has deterred much further publication about the issue, but I believe many theologians share his opinion. What's more, the conviction that every baptised person can and should – in special circumstances – preside at the Eucharist lies embedded in many Catholics' *sense of faith*. Consider this:

The Australian Sister Irene McCormack was born in 1938. In 1956 she joined the Sisters of Saint Joseph. She graduated from university, worked as a teacher and then as a principal of a school. In 1987 she was sent as a missionary to a small inland diocese in Peru. She worked there both in education and as a Eucharistic minister in local parish churches. The problem at the time was that the countryside was ravaged by terrorists belonging to the so-called "Shining Path." In 1989 she was moved to the village of Huasahuasi. To make a long story short, when assaults by the terrorists increased, the two local priests left the area. Irene and some companions decided to stay in loyalty to the local people. She was assassinated in May of 1991.

When priests were absent, Irene used to preside at local Eucharists, first during para-liturgies, but then at "real Masses." I presume she would speak the words of consecration. And she has left us some powerful testimonies about this in her correspondence.

This is what she wrote on July 17, 1990, in the year before her death:

> Have given up trying to use the terms "para-liturgy" or "liturgy of the Word" or any other "excuses" the official church uses to deny collaborative ministry its rightful place to women and married lay people. I used to try to do the "right" thing and correct the people when they came asking us to celebrate their "Masses." I've become convinced that they are closer to the truth and were "freeing" me to exercise eucharistic ministry amongst them....

> It seems to me, therefore, that the preoccupation of our Church leaders with power and control over who can celebrate the Eucharist, who can and who can't receive the Eucharist, is right up the creek. It's a contradiction to be talking about a "sacred meal," and have to sit and watch, not participate.... Not only is it a contradiction to the proclamation of Jesus that there is no distinction between male and female, but a lack of appreciation of the plight of villagers like ours all over the world, that our Church continue denying in its official ministry that it is by nature "communion".... Reflecting on the experience afterwards, I felt much more in touch with what the Last Supper and the Eucharist were and are about.

> As we in our little Christian communities,

high up in the Andes, gather in memory of Jesus, there is no power or authority on earth that can convince me that Jesus is not personally present.

I feel grateful that these months on end without the "official Mass" and in a culture where I'm experiencing new symbols, has gifted me with a new appreciation of the Eucharist.

I consider Sr. Irene McCormack a true contemporary martyr. And which true Christian would dare to assert that Christ was not fully present when she presided over Eucharists for her people – simply "because she was only a woman, and women cannot be priests"?

Did the Spirit not act and speak in Sister Irene, revealing the mind of Christ?

Chapter 9

Women deacons of the past

For a thousand years, the Church ordained
women to the diaconate.

During the first thousand years of its
existence, the Church regularly ordained
women as deacons, receiving them into Holy
Orders. The orders of deacon and priest are part of
the same sacrament, and so by extension it is clear
that women can receive priestly ordination as well.

The Early Church knew many kinds of ministers.
But from quite early on it distinguished the "higher
orders" (diaconate, priesthood and episcopacy)
from the "lower orders" (doorkeepers, acolytes,
readers, etc.). The higher orders were conferred by
the imposition of hands and the calling down of
the Holy Spirit. The lower orders by a blessing in
the sacristy.

There is mounting evidence from literature and iconography that women ministered as priests in some ancient Christian communities. But for now, let's focus on the indisputable fact that women were ordained deacons for a thousand years in all known Christian countries of the time. If we were to visit the eastern Mediterranean during that time, we would find a female deacon in virtually every parish.

In the fifth century, for instance, you could meet deacons Theodosia in Edessa, Celerina in Constantinople, and Publia in Antioch – not to mention the other 110 women deacons we know by name from letters and tombstones. You would discover that they exercised an important ministry in their local communities.

The tasks of a female deacon

An example of a woman deacon's contribution to the local parish can be seen in sixth-century Deacon Maria of Archelaïs in Cappadocia. We read on her tombstone:

> Here lies Maria the deacon of pious and blessed memory who, faithful to the saying of the Apostle, raised children, exercised hospitality, washed the feet of the saints, and distributed her bread to the needy. Remember her, Lord, when she enters into your kingdom.

Her community obviously remembered her as a kind and loving person. She must also have been in good standing and reasonably well off. From the tributes given we can reconstruct what she did for people. She visited the sick in their homes and cared for them. She looked after abandoned or neglected children. She provided shelter to the homeless. She distributed food to the poor. Small wonder people loved her.

One of the key functions of a woman deacon was to assist in the baptism of women. During the first millennium more and more people joined the Christian community. Adult baptism was the norm, and female ministers were needed to help perform the rite. The church laws of Justinian (535 A.D.) describe the task of the woman deacon as "ministering to the revered rites of Baptism and to be part of other hidden rites, which they rightly perform in connection with the venerable mysteries." The *Didascalia of the Apostles* (250 A.D.) gives this instruction to bishops:

> When women go down into the water [of the baptismal font], it is necessary that those going down into the water be anointed with the oil of anointing by a woman deacon.... It is not good for women to be seen [naked] by a man.

In those early centuries, baptism was *the* major sacrament leading up to participation in the Eucharist. When people applied for admission to the Church, Deacon Maria would be given charge of teaching and preparing the women catechumens.

This would often also involve visits to their homes.

After months of instruction, punctuated by exorcism sessions and rites of initiation, catechumens would be ready for the actual baptism on the Saturday vigil before Easter. Again, there were introductory rites. When the actual baptism started, the men would first be ministered to by the parish priest and male deacon. Then it would be the turn for the women.

Now Deacon Maria would take charge. She would lead the women to the priest who would anoint the first female catechumen with a sign of the cross on her forehead, saying a prayer such as, "Be anointed [name] with the oil of gladness which overcomes all violence of the enemy and by which you will be protected in the name of the Father, the Son and the Holy Spirit." Then Deacon Maria would take the catechumen into the baptistry itself, which was an enclosure round a small pond: the baptismal font. Three steps would lead into the middle of the font.

Deacon Maria would strip the catechumen of all her clothes and ornaments. She would untie the woman's hair "to ensure that nothing partaking of an alien spirit should descend with her into the water of second birth." Maria would then anoint the naked catechumen over every part of her body. The anointing was itself an exorcism, implying a healing from all evil related to the body.

Maria would now lead the naked catechumen down the steps, from the west to the east, so that the catechumen faced east. In the middle the font was about waist-deep. Maria would descend into the font with her. The priest – standing behind a curtain so as not to see the naked woman – would usually speak the Trinitarian formula. Meanwhile Deacon Maria would immerse the catechumen three times, hand on her head: "I baptise this handmaid of God [*name*] in the name of the Father" – *first immersion* – "and the Son" – *second immersion* – "and the Holy Spirit" – *third immersion.*

In some areas, we know, the woman deacon herself performed "both the anointing and the baptism."

Maria would now help the newly baptised woman climb out of the font, walking towards the east – resurrection! There Maria would "receive her," in the words of the ancient texts. This meant: dry her with a towel.

Again, we should appreciate the exhilarating experience for the newly baptised. Maria would gently rub her limbs dry, seeing to it that the oil that had soaked into the skin would still cling to it, making the neophyte feel healthy and whole and new all over.

Maria would now dress her in a white robe, saying, "The handmaid of God [*name*] is clothed with the garment of righteousness, in the name of the Father, the Son and the Holy Spirit." Then Maria would bring her to the priest. The priest would make a sign of the cross on her forehead with holy chrism, a special oil mixed with herbs and blessed for this purpose, saying, "The seal of the gift of the Holy Spirit!"

Maria would continue to minister to the women. At the Sunday Eucharist she would welcome them at the church door and conduct them to their places. She would visit them at home, take them Holy Communion when they were ill, administer Extreme Unction if needed, and help the family prepare for their funerals when they died.

Deacon Maria provided many services, but it was principally for her role in Baptism that she had been ordained. A version of the ordination prayer found in the Eastern European country of Georgia illuminates this point further:

> Promote this your handmaid to the ministry, that she may anoint the women that come to your holy Baptism with oil and bring them to your holy font, so that she may become a deacon of your church, according to the order of Phoebe, whom the apostle [Paul] ordained as minister....

Women deacons received a sacramental ordination

Ordination rites for women deacons have been preserved in both the Greek-speaking East and Latin-speaking West. Let's focus on the Eastern rite, which has been preserved in more detail. The oldest form is found in the *Apostolic Constitutions* (A.D. 380), then in major manuscripts from the eighth, ninth and tenth centuries. All these written parchments contain basically the same rite, tracing back to Constantinople in the fifth century.

The rite describes how, in the middle of the Eucharistic celebration, before the offertory begins, the female candidate is brought up to the bishop's throne in front of the sanctuary. The bishop introduces the candidate by name to the congregation and designates her for the diaconate ministry in a particular parish. This is known as the "Divine Grace" statement, which preceded all major ordinations.

> Divine Grace, which always heals what is infirm and makes up for what is lacking, promotes [*name of person*] to be deacon [*or priest, bishop*] in [*name of place*]. Let us therefore pray that the grace of the Holy Spirit may descend on him/her.

The candidate bends her head before the bishop. He imposes his hand on her head and invokes the Holy Spirit on her:

> Holy and omnipotent Lord, through the birth of your only Son our God from a virgin according to the flesh, you have sanctified the female sex. You grant not only to men, but also to women the grace and coming of the Holy Spirit. Please, Lord, look on this your maid servant and dedicate her to the task of your diaconate. Pour out into her the rich and abundant giving of your Holy Spirit. Preserve her so that she may always perform her

ministry with orthodox faith and irreproachable conduct, according to what is pleasing to you. For to you is due all glory and honour.

Then, while the congregation prays the intercessions, the bishop performs a second imposition of hands. This was done in all major ordinations. Imposing his hand on her head, the bishop says:

> Lord, Master, you do not reject women who dedicate themselves to you and who are willing, in a becoming way, to serve your Holy House, but admit them to the order of your ministers. Grant the gift of your Holy Spirit also to this your maid servant who wants to dedicate herself to you, and fulfill in her the grace of the diaconate, as you have granted to Phoebe the grace of your diaconate, whom you had called to the work of the ministry. Give her, Lord, that she may persevere without guilt in your Holy Temple, that she may carefully guard her behaviour, especially her modesty and temperance. Moreover, make your maid servant perfect, so that, when she will stand before the judgment seat of your Christ, she may obtain the worthy fruit of her excellent conduct, through the mercy and humanity of your only Son.

Notice how in both ordination prayers the Holy Spirit is called down on the woman to make her a deacon. These are exactly the same formulas used for male deacons. In fact, the ordination prayers for men and women are identical apart from Stephen being held out as the model for the men (Acts 6,5-14) and Phoebe as the one for women (Rom 16,1-2).

The same applies to other significant elements of the ordination rite. The newly ordained woman deacon, just like her male counterpart, received the diaconate stole which, we know, only *true deacons* were allowed to wear under pain of excommunication. At the time of Holy Communion the bishop himself offered her the sacred body and precious blood, as he did to the male deacon. Then the bishop handed her the chalice, which she took back to the altar with her own hands. This indicated that as a deacon she had *the power* to handle the sacred vessels, even though in public celebrations it was usually the male deacons who distributed communion. The woman deacon took communion to the sick.

The Church affirmed women's openness to full ordination

In 1563, the Council of Trent declared that the sacrament of Holy Orders establishes a hierarchy of bishops, priests and deacons. It reiterated that the sacrament had been instituted by Christ himself. Vatican II confirmed *the unity of the sacrament* by speaking of one "divinely established ministry which is exercised on different levels by those who from antiquity have been called bishops, priests and deacons."

Scholars have pointed out the significance of the Vatican Council's teaching: The diaconate and the priesthood belong to the same sacrament. And scholars take it further:

"If women have been ordained deacons, the unity of the sacrament of Holy Orders demands their access to the sacramental priesthood."

For me, this means the bishops who ordained women to be deacons implicitly affirmed their openness to the priesthood. Remember this phrase in the ordination prayer:

"Through the birth of your only Son our God from a virgin according to the flesh, *you have sanctified the female sex. You grant not only to men, but also to women the grace and coming of the Holy Spirit.*"

It is a general principle. Women, too, have been sanctified. They, too, can receive the Holy Spirit in sacramental ordination.

Why should this be limited to the diaconate only?

During the first millennium throughout the Middle East, bishops ordained tens of thousands of women deacons. They all expressed the same principle – bishops in Italy and Syria, bishops in Crete and Asia Minor, bishops in Sicily, Egypt and Greece.

Was it not the mind of Christ speaking through them?

It is crystal clear, therefore, that Jesus Christ also sanctified the female sex. Women, too, can receive the grace and coming of the Holy Spirit in sacramental ordination, including the priesthood.

Chapter 10

The Catholic *sense of faith*

This source of infallible knowledge affirms
that women can be priests.

How do we know what truly belongs to our Catholic faith?

Is it only what priests, bishops or the Pope tell us? No. An important source of knowledge lies in our hearts and minds. It has been called the "sense of faith," the "Gospel in the heart," the "Catholic sense," the "ecclesiastical spirit," the "sense of the church," and sometimes the "consensus of the church." And by "church" is meant the whole community of believers.

Tradition has always stressed the crucial role which the *sense of faith* plays in the life of the Church. For this sense of faith is truly alive and aware.

The sense of faith in our hearts does not carry only a bundle of old truths. Under guidance of the Spirit, it tests new developments and it assesses their value. We come across new problems and fresh possibilities, which makes our faith blossom with an enriched vision that leads to adaptation and growth. This makes Christian Tradition a *living* tradition, alive because it opens up to wider horizons while facing questions that need answering.

The sense of faith is the people of God's awareness, an ever-renewed awareness – and it has always known that women can be ministerial priests.

The faithful speak up

Some years ago, I visited a friend named Clara in the Netherlands. She teaches religious education in a secondary school. On Sundays she reads at Mass and helps in distributing communion. She was upset.

"Our parish priest says that it was Jesus who barred women from ordination," she told me. "Apparently that's what the Pope has said. But I can't believe it. Surely not Jesus! I can't see for the life of me why *Jesus* would not want us women to preach or to be the main celebrant at Mass!"

She is right, of course. And she is not alone. The vast majority of Catholics in countries where people have been educated see no problem in women being ordained. Seventy percent of American Catholics support the ordination of women. So do Catholics in France (83%), Spain (78%), Argentina (60%), Italy (59%) and Brazil (54%). Whereas in Poland the percentage was still 11% in 1999, in 2014 it had risen to 38% – and that in spite of admiration for the Polish Pope, John Paul II, and intense indoctrination by the hierarchy. In the Netherlands support reaches well over 90%, and this is also among religious sisters, catechists, pastoral workers and parish councillors.

Now, we are not talking here of deciding the contents of doctrine by democratic vote. But it is very telling that so many Catholics in all these countries who have little or no contact with each other think alike. They are expressing their honest feelings. As in this letter I received from San Francisco:

"I have a master's in liturgical studies and am choir director in my parish. I give workshops for lectors and cantors. I believe to the core of my being that women should be ordained. I don't know how much longer I'll be able to be a Catholic with a straight face...."

Is this not the *sense of faith*, Catholic awareness, the Spirit of Christ himself speaking?

And this is not a small matter. As Vatican II teaches, the Church is "inerrant" in faith. This means it cannot hold a falsehood as true doctrine. And this "inerrancy" is rooted in the universal *sense of faith* carried by the faithful:

The body of the faithful as a whole, anointed as they are by the Holy One (cf. 1 John 2,20.27), cannot err in matters of belief. Thanks to a supernatural *sense of the faith* which characterizes the People as a whole, it manifests this unerring quality when 'from the bishops down to the last member of the laity,' it shows universal agreement in matters of faith and morals. For, by this *sense of faith* which is aroused and sustained by the Spirit of truth, God's People accept not the word of human beings, but the very Word of God (cf. 1 Thessalonians 2,13). It clings without fail to the faith once delivered to the saints, penetrates it more deeply by accurate insights, and applies it more thoroughly to life.

Ah!, you may say, *but the Pope and bishops know best!*

Not necessarily so. The people of God's *sense of faith* is the primary source of both the Church's inerrancy and the infallibility enjoyed by Church authorities (ecumenical councils, the world epis-copate, or the Pope) when they, fulfilling the right conditions, make a decisive pronouncement on doctrine.

The Pope and the college of bishops no doubt have a crucial role in articulating matters of faith and morals through their authoritative teaching. However, this exercise *is grounded in* the infallibility of the whole people of God, not the other way around. A proposal during Vatican II that wanted to make the infallibility of the *magisterium* the source of the people's infallibility was rejected by the Vatican Council as being contrary to Tradition.

Testimonies of the faithful in the past

Before we proceed to actual manifestations of the *sense of faith*, it is crucial to grasp that the faithful may carry a belief *implicitly*. They may not be conscious of it, though it is part of their deep inner convictions. The *sense of faith* lies deeply embedded in the hearts and minds of the faithful. Some issues come into the conscious mind only when changing circumstances draw them out. This is why the *sense of faith* is also called "latent" – that is, "hidden" – tradition.

The great theologian Saint Cardinal John Henry Newman explained implicit, latent tradition in these words:

> Now, it is important to insist on the reality and permanence of inward knowledge, as distinct from explicit confession. The absence, or partial absence, or incompleteness of dogmatic statements is no proof of the absence of beliefs or implicit judgments, in the mind of the Church. Even centuries might pass without the formal expression of a truth which had been all along the secret life of millions of faithful souls.

An example of such a latent tradition can be seen in our belief in the Blessed Trinity: one God in three persons. During the first three centuries after Christ, the doctrine did not exist in explicit form. It is only at the Council of Nicea in 325 A.D. that the doctrine was explicitly expressed in the form with which we are familiar today. In previous centuries the doctrine lay hidden in people's *sense of faith*. It was implicitly contained in their prayers and in the practice of baptising people "in the name of the Father, the Son and the Holy Spirit." It was the threat of the Arian heresy which reduced Christ to a secondary status that forced the members of the Council of Nicea to clearly define the relationship of Father, Son and Spirit in the trinitarian creed, so well known to us today.

Now, notice that baptism "in the name of the Father, the Son and the Holy Spirit" was an external "indicator" that revealed the trinitarian belief held in people's hearts by the *sense of faith*.

When it comes to the ordination of women, indicators of latent belief in the ability of women to function as priests can be seen in a remarkable ancient devotion to the Virgin Mary as a priest.

Devotion to Mary Priest

For 16 centuries, from around 300 A.D. until 1927 – when it was suddenly prohibited – millions of Catholics venerated Mary, the mother of Jesus, as a priest.

The devotion began with the Fathers of the Church who hailed Mary as being of priestly descent. They called her the New Testament's "altar of holocausts," "the ark of the new covenant," the "sacrificial priest." Mary's priesthood was further elaborated upon by theologians in the Middle Ages. It blossomed in the writings of sixteenth through nineteenth century theologians, especially in Italy, Spain, France and Germany. It was universally recognized by bishops, cardinals and popes.

This was a truly massive devotional phenomenon. Devotees stressed Mary's involvement in the sacrifice on Calvary and in the Eucharist.

• "Mary was priestess ... she stood by the Cross ... to offer the Son of God for the salvation of the world." (St. Antoninus, 1389-1459)

• "The most blessed Virgin fulfilled the function of priest because ... she offered and sacrificed her Son on the altar of the cross ... just as she offers every day with the priests the body of her Son in the non-bloody sacrifice of the most holy Eucharist." (Ferdinand de Salazar, 1575-1646)

• "Mary is no stranger in anything that belongs to the Eucharist. She was the first priest to call down the Word from heaven to earth.... She was the first sacrificer as she had been the first consecrator ... on top of the holy mount of Calvary...." (Bishop Morelle, 1911)

Mary's priesthood was also celebrated in images. We find Mary wearing an episcopal pallium on frescoes in many ancient churches, such as San Vincenzo, San Venanzio and Santa Maria Antica in Rome. On paintings in German, French and Spanish churches Mary is portrayed standing before the altar in priestly vestments. In 1906, Pope Leo XIII received "with joy" a painting of Our Lady in priestly vestments.

But did this devotion not raise questions? Theologians of the seventeenth and nineteenth centuries defended and explained the concept:

• "The glorious Virgin was anointed not externally but interiorly. She was ordained a priest, not according to the law, but according to the Spirit."

• "Mary has been anointed and ordained by the Holy Spirit himself."

• "Although she was a woman, the Blessed Virgin carried all the invisible grace of the apostles and priests in herself. She had already been ordained with the fullness of grace."

In 1906, Pope Pius X still attached a 300-days' indulgence to a prayer addressing Mary Priest. But ten years later, in 1916, the Holy Office forbade the use of images of Mary portraying her as a priest. And then, in 1927, under Pope Pius XI, the entire devotion was abruptly forbidden: "The Holy Office no longer wants any question of a devotion to the Virgin Priest." The reason was obviously that under guidance of the World Council of Churches more and more Christian denominations were beginning to admit women to full participation in the ministry.

But Rome's sudden action could not wipe out the voice of Catholic consciousness during the 16 preceding centuries.

By venerating Mary as priest – in fact, as the Catholic priest *par excellence* – the faithful strongly affirmed that women can be priests. Thus, the *sense of faith* had revealed the mind of Christ.

In summary...

As we have seen, the root of the Church's infallibility lies deep in the hearts of the Christian community. This truth is borne out by the Vatican II document *Lumen Gentium:*

> The body of the faithful as a whole, anointed as they are by the Holy One, cannot err in matters of belief. Thanks to a supernatural *sense of the faith* which characterizes the People as a whole...

Throughout the history of the Church, the faithful have known, in their heart of hearts, that women can be ordained priests. This belief lay implicitly contained in the widespread devotion to the Blessed Virgin as the ideal model for Catholic priesthood.

In our own days, the scales have fallen away from the eyes of the faithful. Educated Catholics all over the world now realise that women were excluded from the priesthood because of the overpowering bias against women in all spheres of life. They now demand that women be admitted to Holy Orders. The *sense of faith* has spoken. Catholics are clearly speaking their minds.

This is the Spirit, revealing and strongly affirming the mind of Christ.

Chapter 11

The Church's error in condoning slavery

As with slavery, the Church should admit its past mistakes regarding the treatment of women.

For centuries, Church authorities have inflicted a great injustice on women by excluding them from their rightful share in priestly ministry. In recent decades popes have made matters even worse by issuing hefty statements to bolster that injustice, as if such statements were part of Catholic doctrine.

Indeed, Pope John Paul II proclaimed in a 1995 letter titled *Responsum ad Dubium* (translated: Response to a doubt) that the Church's decision not to ordain women is "to be held always, everywhere, and by all, as *belonging to the deposit of the faith.*" He attempted to nail the papal colours to this archaic patriarchal practice.

Some years ago, I had a bit of a debate with a parish priest who was against women's ordination.

"If what you say is true," he remarked to me, "if women can be ordained as priests, think of the damage it would do to the authority of the Church."

"The Church is doing much more damage to itself by not honestly admitting it has made a mistake," I replied. I also pointed out Jesus' condemnation of the scribes and pharisees for "tying up heavy burdens, hard to bear, and laying them on people's shoulders."

Should Church authorities not be more concerned about the welfare of the faithful, rather than on maintaining a rigorous front on out-of-date rules and practices?

The Church has made mistakes in the past, costly mistakes that deeply affected the lives of people. Condoning slavery was one such mistake. We should learn from this.

Why did the Church ignore the cries of slaves?

The fundamental right of one person to own another as slave was accepted and endorsed by Hebrew law. Slaves were protected by law in certain cases, as we have seen in the books of Exodus and Deuteronomy. If a slave belonged to a Jewish person, the slave had the right of being liberated in a number of circumstances. The institution of slavery itself, however, was not questioned. Before telling masters how to treat their slaves, Sirach bases the inequality of free people and slaves on a disposition of God himself – similar to the way some blame Christ for excluding women from the priesthood.

This social myth of slavery was still very much in force at the time of Christ. He himself does not contradict it in any single text; in fact, he introduced slaves into his parables for the sake of comparison. We are told to be like slaves that are faithful to their master even when the master is not at home. Jesus viewed slavery as a reality in his own time.

During the few years of his public ministry, Jesus could not bring about the radical social reforms inherent in his vision, for it takes decades, if not centuries, to accomplish such a major cultural shift.

Nor was the eradication of slavery a goal of the Early Church. The apostles instructed their Christian slaves to be obedient to their masters, not to rebel against them. Consider these passages:

• "Slaves must be respectful and obedient to their masters, not only when they are kind and gentle but also when they are unfair." (1 Pet 2, 18-20)

• "Slaves, be obedient to the men who are called your masters in this world, with deep respect and sincere loyalty, as you are obedient to Christ."

(Eph 6, 5-8; 1 Tim 6, 1-2; Titus 2, 9- 10)

Furthermore, the terminology of slavery is often used in religious symbolism. Redemption is understood as a liberation from the slavery of sin. Even the Incarnation is described as the Son assuming the form of a slave.

Jesus could have spoken out against slavery, but he did not do so. Some may take this to mean that Jesus accepted slavery, and thus condoned it as a permanent norm. (This is the same kind of logic used by those who are steadfast in their opposition to women in the priesthood.) Additionally, the apostles recognised the distinction between masters and slaves as a valid one, with corresponding duties assigned to each according to his status. Such were the arguments of traditional theology that remained unchallenged until abolitionists forced the Church to re-examine its doctrine on the matter.

But the Church should have listened to the cries of people much earlier.

The first real opportunity to challenge the institution of slavery came during Paul's lifetime. A slave called Onesimos escaped from his master in the Greek city of Ephesus and fled to Rome, where Paul had been imprisoned. That is where Paul baptised him. Then Paul sent him back to Ephesus, asking his master to grant him his liberty, for only slave owners could set their slaves free, by Roman law:

"Receive him no longer as a slave but more than a slave – as a beloved brother."

Paul went even further in a letter to the Galatians in which he stated a general principle with major implications for the Church for all time:

> For all of you who were baptized into Christ have clothed yourselves with Christ. There is no longer Jew or Greek, slave or free, male or female. You are all one in Christ.

Paul had listened to Onesimos. He had grasped *in principle* that insertion into Christ's Kingdom of God implied liberation from slavery. But few followed his insight. Christians continued to keep and buy slaves.

Three centuries later, St. Gregory, Bishop of Nyssa, raised his voice in protest. He advocated the total abolition of slavery. "To own people is to buy the image of God," he taught.

Gregory records that in his cathedral slaves were released from their bondage on the day of Easter "according to the custom of the Church." And he pleaded for Christians to listen to their consciences:

> You condemn a person to slavery who by nature is free and independent, and so you make laws opposed to God and to his natural law. For you have subjected to the yoke of slavery a person who was made precisely to be lord of the earth and whom the Creator intended to be a ruler, thus resisting and rejecting his divine precept.

Have you forgotten what limits were set to your authority? God limited your ownership only to brute animals.

Who gave heed to his voice?

Not the official Church. Church synods decreed that slavery could be imposed as a penalty on vicious or stupid people. The Synod of Melfi under Pope Urban II in 1089 – I write this with tears in my eyes – imposed slavery on the wives of priests. It also stipulated that, whereas ordinary slaves could be bought free, the former wives of priests could never be redeemed. Who would listen to their cries?

Medieval theologians like Thomas Aquinas defended slavery as instituted by God in punishment for sin. He considered slavery to be part of the "right of nations" and natural law. He attempted to justify slavery in these categories: penal enslavement; captured in conquest; people who sold themselves to pay off debts, or who were sold by a court for that reason. Children born of a slave mother are rightly slaves, he taught, even though they have not committed personal sin!

Another true Christian spoke out in 1550. It was the Dominican friar Bartolomé de las Casas. Working as a missionary in Peru, he saw native tribespeople being herded out of their villages and forced to work on plantations. He witnessed African slaves being unloaded from their slave ships and sold as cattle on the common market. These men and women had been bought from human traffickers in Nigeria and Senegal. He tended their wounds. He saw the despair in their eyes. He took their case to the Catholic King of Spain in Valladolid and pleaded for their release:

> Our Christian religion is suitable for, and may be adapted to all the nations of the world, and all alike can receive it.... No single person may be deprived of his liberty. Are these tribals not people like us? Do they not have rational souls? Are we not obliged to love them as we love ourselves?

Unfortunately, the Church refused to listen. It gave in to slave traders and their colonial overlords. The popes, who should have been champions of the underdogs, endorsed the theory and practice of slavery.

In 1454, Pope Nicholas V sanctioned the practice of enslaving people of conquered nations, including Muslims.

In 1493, Alexander VI authorised the King of Spain to enslave non-Christians of the Americas who were at war with Christianity.

In 1548, Paul III re-stated the principle that citizens and members of the clergy could own slaves.

And even though in later centuries a succession of popes were to denounce the slave trade of Negroes from Africa, slavery as such was tolerated.

In 1866, another opportunity arose. Bishops in Ethiopia were concerned about the condition of slaves. "Is slavery in harmony with Catholic doctrine?" they asked. Remember, by that time slavery had already been abolished in most civilised countries, including the colonial powers of Britain, the Netherlands, France and Spain. But Pius IX, after condemning injustices committed against individual slaves, re-affirmed the principle:

> Slavery itself, considered as such in its essential nature, is *not at all contrary to the natural and divine law,* and there can be several just titles of slavery and these are referred to by approved theologians and commentators of the sacred canons.... It is not contrary to the natural and divine law for a slave to be sold, bought, exchanged or given....

It took time for the Church to come to its senses. In 1891, 25 years after Pius IX's proclamation, Pope Leo XIII issued the encyclical *Rerum Novarum* (translated: On new developments) in which any legitimate excuse for slavery was denied. In 1918, the new Code of Canon Law imposed heavy ecclesiastical penalties on whoever "sells a human being into slavery." And in 1965, the Second Vatican Council stated:

> All offences against human dignity: such as... arbitrary imprisonment, deportation, slavery... the traffic in women and children... all these and the like are criminal. They poison civilisation; and they debase the perpetrators more than the victims and militate against the honour of the Creator.

But did these retractions of doctrine not come

centuries and centuries too late? What about the millions of men, women and children who had been deprived of their human dignity and subjected to lives of utter misery because the official Church did not stand up for them? Will not Christ at the Last Judgment say, "I was a slave and you did not untie my bonds"?

Church leaders must understand that they have a real responsibility for people's welfare and that they can't escape Christ's judgment on this. The United Kingdom and the United States outlawed the international slave trade in 1807, the Netherlands in 1814. Britain abolished slavery throughout its empire in 1833, the French colonies abolished it in 1848, and the U.S. abolished it in 1865. While prophetic theologians and others were clamouring for the Church to support abolition, Church leaders ignored the human desperation of the poor slaves and defended the principle of slavery.

In a very similar way, modern-day Church leaders are trying to suppress the voices of those who are speaking up against another unconscionable, age-old injustice: the exclusion of women from the priesthood.

Chapter 12

Jesus wants women in the priesthood

In our own time, the Spirit calls out
for the Church to ordain women.

During bygone centuries, Christian communities were engulfed by the social climate in which they lived, so ordaining women was out of the question. But in our own time, there are no further excuses for this kind of discrimination. It is clear that ordaining women is in full accord with the mind of Christ.

Today, as in the past, millions upon millions of Catholics suffer because women are denied full access to service in the priesthood.

We all know that Jesus lived two millennia ago in Palestine. During his short, three-year public ministry, he revealed his Father's new kingdom of love, a vision that would revolutionise the history of humankind. But 2,000 years ago, Jesus's audience was not capable of understanding all the implications of his message. In fact, Jesus himself could not imagine the full future extent of the religious and social revolution he was bringing about, limited as he was in his human form. John's Gospel tells us that Jesus foresaw this problem and provided a solution.

"I will ask the Father, and he will send you someone else as Counsellor to be with you forever, the Spirit of Truth....

"I have said these things to you while still with you. But the Counsellor, the Holy Spirit, whom the Father will send in my name, will teach you everything and remind you of everything I have said to you."

In other words: *Although I will be physically absent, I will continue to guide you through the Spirit. The Spirit in your hearts and minds will explain to you what I had in mind.*

Ah! But what about totally new developments? you might ask. *New insights, new discoveries, new challenges of our own time? Do we have to work them out on our own?*

Yes and no. Jesus might answer. *Yes, because you will have to use your own intelligence and listen to the sense of faith in your heart. No, because you will not face that challenge alone. The Spirit will steer you to the right answer even when brand-new questions arise.*

In John's Gospel, Jesus makes it clear that the Spirit will reveal things to us that he himself didn't.

"I still have many things to say to you but they would be too much for you now. When the Spirit of Truth comes he will lead you to the fullness of truth.... He will explain to you things that lie in the future."

And the Spirit of Christ is speaking to us now – loudly and clearly.

By denying ordination to women the Church does harm to people

Church authorities keep saying that excluding women from ordination is not a question of equality. Women are equal, they say, not only in the eyes of God but also in the eyes of the Church. But that, of course, is simply not true. Leadership in the Church is exercised by priests, bishops, cardinals, the Pope. Barring women from such leadership positions sends a powerful message of factual inequality.

In response to Pope John Paul II's *Ordinatio Sacerdotalis* (translated: On priestly ordination), issued in 1994, 14 theologically qualified religious sisters from India wrote to the Pope:

> There are some statements in your letter that are extremely painful for us to read. No. 1, para. 2 says: 'The Church's teaching authority has

constantly held that the exclusion of women from priesthood is in accordance with God's plan for the Church.' The phrase 'exclusion of women' seems to negate our very membership in the Church. We do have full membership in the Church through the sacraments of initiation, namely Baptism, Confirmation and the Eucharist.

Then why should we as a class be prevented from certain functions in the Church?

Dear Father, who decides what is God's plan for the Church? Is it not the people of God? Do you as the father of this family of faithful exclude us from the people of God even in the common search for God's will for the Church today?

Women's inequality-in-fact in the Catholic Church also impedes the vital work of social emancipation. Twenty-seven Christian charity workers in Malaysia gave this testimony:

We live in a culture where boy babies are preferred to girl babies; boys are given preference in education; girls are brutally raped and murdered; women are abused in the family; women are forced into prostitution to provide for the needs of the family; women are rarely consulted or involved in decision-making....

We desperately need a change in mindset of both men and women to bring about a just society. Just as the Catholic Church is recognised for its leadership on issues of justice and solidarity with the poor, it is in a similar position of leadership and influence for the eradication of oppression of women. The Catholic Church would once again be able to assume such a position of leadership with the ordination of women to the priesthood.

When women are admitted into the priesthood in the Catholic Church, its teaching that women and men are both equally made in the image of God would be credible.

More than anything else, by forbidding women to enter the priesthood the Church is depriving millions of Catholics of access to the sacraments. Vocations are dwindling in the West. Priests are forced to continue ministering well past retirement age – with huge costs to the quality of their service. Parishes are being closed and lumped together, which makes it hard for people to go to church especially in rural districts. The discrimination against women increases the large number of Catholics who are more and more being alienated.

With their female charisms and social skills women would also significantly improve the Church's pastoral care for people. In fact, are the colossal blunders committed by the Catholic hierarchy – the child sex abuse scandal and coverup, the condoning of slavery, and others – not the products of a hard-hearted, patriarchal institution? If priests and bishops had been married and if women had ranked in the ministry, the approach might have been more intelligent and caring.

Young girls find it hard to confide their problems to grown-up men. One such girl wrote:

"Already when I had to make my first confession, I felt a deep desire to speak to a female priest. I knew I would have revealed myself so much more easily to a woman than to a man since a man does not understand the fears and worries of a small girl .... The woman whom I sought in my spiritual need did not exist."

Female priests would often be able to reach out to people where men cannot. In Muslim regions, for instance, such as in Pakistan, Indonesia and the Philippines, only women can enter women's quarters. A religious sister who works as a full-time chaplain in a large Dutch hospital reported that some patients in her care died without being able to go to confession or receive the last sacraments because no male priest could be summoned in time. If she had been ordained, she could have provided that service.

Should the spiritual welfare of every single person not be a top priority for the Church?

A religious sister in Africa, looking after a remote community, shared her anguish:

> I resent it more and more, and with ever greater sorrow, that I cannot respond fully to all the needs of people in their searching for God. I am thinking of those people who have not seen a priest in many years, those who during the course of a confidential talk confess their sins spontaneously. I would like so much to be able to give them the sacramental sign of forgiveness there and then! And on Sundays, rather than just handing out communion I would like to respond fully to their spiritual need by renewing Christ's

Eucharistic gesture, the living memorial of his love and his sacrifice.

"Our hands are tied," I hear church authorities grumble. "Jesus himself did not want women to be priests!"

This is an excuse that has been exposed as a fake. Jesus chose twelve men to be the twelve patriarchs of the new Israel. In doing so he never intended to exclude women forever. Moreover, Jesus's true intentions emerge from his respect for women. By welcoming women through the same baptism as men, he opened the door for their entering his new priesthood. When instituting the Eucharist, he said also to women: "Do this in memory of me!" Christians through the centuries have understood Christ's mind by admiring Mary of Magdala as the "Apostle of the Apostles," and by venerating Jesus' mother Mary as sharing in his priesthood. For centuries the Church admitted women to the sacrament of Holy Orders by ordaining women, as much as men, to the diaconate.

Blaming Jesus for the exclusion of women is not a valid excuse. Plain patriarchal prejudice has been the real culprit.

The Church should now listen to the Spirit crying out in people. For through that Spirit Christ is revealing his mind: *My people need the ministry of women. I want women, too, to be priests. I want it now, without further excuses or delays.*

Appendix 1

Papal documents opposing the ordination of women

The question of the ordination of women has preoccupied Church authorities since the 1960s and '70s. Four popes have been involved: Paul VI, John Paul II, Benedict XVI and now Francis. Pressures have come both from ecumenism – other Christian churches beginning to ordain women – and from women's groups within the Catholic Church.

Documents show that the thinking in the Vatican has fluctuated a good deal on *why* women have been excluded from the priesthood. But there seems to have been no willingness to budge on the issue itself – predictably so, in light of decades of traditionalists' hold on the papacy. Women *cannot* be priests, it is claimed. And the reason? The exclusion must go back to Jesus himself. It is Jesus who made that decision for all times, and the Church cannot go against that edict, Church authorities claim. When Jesus established his new ministerial priesthood, he established one in which – intentionally – women have no place, they maintain.

No 1. *Inter Insigniores* **("Among the Most Significant")** **– October 15, 1976.** "Declaration of the Sacred Congregation for the Doctrine of the Faith on the question of the admission of women to the ministerial priesthood."

No 2. Commentary on *Inter Insigniores* – January 27, 1977 – by the Sacred Congregation for the Doctrine of the Faith.

These two complementary documents, issued under the papacy of Pope Paul VI, were the Catholic Church's official reaction to other Christian Churches beginning to ordain women. In this section, I summarise their contents in as succinct a manner as possible. I re-word them in my own way, quoting key passages from the text itself in their identical words whenever possible:

All over the world women are gradually assuming their rightful place in society. In the Church, too, women are taking a more active role in various forms of the apostolate. The Church is happy about this. The Vatican always lays great stress on the need of taking away all forms of discrimination against women.

Side by side with this good development of women's emancipation, however, there is one trend that gives cause for alarm. This is the expectation now found with many that one day women too will be admitted to the ministerial priesthood. The ordination of women in Protestant Churches, and especially in Churches belonging to the Anglican communion, has helped to strengthen similar hopes in Catholic circles. Before things get out of hand, one should realise that doctrinally there is no place for women priests in the Catholic Church. This should not be understood as a form of discrimination. It is simply a factual decision in the plan of salvation that priests should be chosen from among men, not from among women.

It is true there is no explicit teaching in Scripture

that restricts the priesthood only to men. How then, you may ask, can we deduce that women are excluded from the ministry? Such a conclusion can be arrived at, with practical certainty, from the combination of the following facts:

1. Jesus Christ chose only men to be his apostles. He obviously did this on purpose and so established a norm.

2. The Church has always followed this example of Christ. Both in apostolic times and in later centuries only men have been ordained priests.

3. A priest is the sacramental sign of Christ's presence at the Eucharist. A man can represent Christ better because Christ, too, was a man.

Christ counted many women among his followers, so he cannot be said to have nurtured the social prejudices to which his contemporaries were subject. He could therefore easily have co-opted some women among his apostolic twelve. Choosing only men must have been a deliberate decision.

The apostles continued the same tradition. To replace Judas, "not Mary, but Matthias was selected to be an apostle." Although many women played leading roles in the foundation of the new Christian communities among the gentiles, no woman was placed in charge of a community as its priest. Paul says that women should not speak in the church assembly (1 Cor 14, 34-35; 1 Tim 2, 12). This does not refer to a passing cultural custom such as wearing a veil on the head (Cor 11, 2-16), but seems to refer to a specific role in the Church permanently reserved to men.

Now, if it was Jesus's wish that only men should be sacramental priests, the Church cannot do anything about it. The Church cannot change the substance of any sacramental sign. Jesus could have chosen various substances to play a role in his sacraments. In reality, he chose water as the instrument of baptism. He chose bread and wine as the matter for the Eucharistic meal. The selection of men for the priesthood must be seen as an equally specific choice of a sacramental sign. The Church cannot depart from norms laid down by Jesus Christ.

Of necessity, the Incarnation took a very specific form. Theoretically speaking, God might have become flesh and lived among us as a woman. Then the whole situation would have been different. As it is, Jesus was a man and therefore it is more natural that he should be sacramentally represented in the Eucharist community by a man. This is also in agreement with general scriptural symbolism according to which Christ is the bridegroom and the community his bride.

"We can never ignore the fact that Christ is a man.... In actions which demand the character of ordination and in which Christ himself, the author of the Covenant, the Bridegroom and Head of the Church, is represented, exercising his ministry of salvation – which is in the highest degree the case in the Eucharist – his role must be taken by a man. This does not stem from any personal superiority of the latter in the order of values, but only from a difference of fact on the level of functions and service."

No 3. *Mulieris Dignitatem* ("A Woman's Dignity") – August 15, 1988. Apostolic Letter of Pope John Paul II "On the Dignity and Vocation of Women."

Throughout this lengthy document, Pope John Paul II extols the inherent dignity of womanhood. He does so at times in terms less acceptable to modern women such as when he says that the highest fulfillment of the female personality lies in virginity or motherhood (*Mulieris* §17). But the most contentious statements in the encyclical concern what John Paul II considers the deepest reason why only men can be ordained priests.

First, the Pope repeats the assertion that Jesus Christ intentionally excluded women from the priesthood: "In calling only men as his Apostles, Christ acted in a completely free and sovereign manner.... The 'Twelve' are with Christ at the Last Supper. They alone receive the sacramental charge, 'Do this in remembrance of me' (Lk 22:19; 1 Cor 11:24), which is joined to the institution of the Eucharist. On Easter Sunday night they receive the Holy Spirit for the forgiveness of sins: 'Whose sins you forgive are forgiven them, and whose sins you retain are retained' (Jn 20:23)." (*Mulieris* §26)

But then the Pope, following the theologian Hans Urs von Balthasar, makes the momentous statement that the distinct roles of man and woman in the Eucharist are embedded in the Incarnation itself. Christ wanted to become human as a male, *as a man.* He redeemed humankind *as a man.* He is present in the Eucharist *as a man.* That is why only men can truly represent him as his priests. The theory is based on a farfetched interpretation of the allegory of Christ the Bridegroom and the Church as his Bride (Eph 5,25-32).

> The Bridegroom – the Son consubstantial with the Father as God – became the Son of Mary. He became the "son of man," *true man, a male.* The symbol of the

Bridegroom is masculine . . . . The Eucharist is the
sacrament of the Bridegroom and the Bride.... Since
Christ, in instituting the Eucharist, linked it in such
an explicit way to the priestly service of the Apostles
[who were all men], it is legitimate to conclude that
he thereby wished to express the relationship between
man and woman, between what is "feminine" and
what is "masculine." It is a relationship willed by God
both in the mystery of creation and in the mystery
of redemption. It is the Eucharist that expresses the
redemptive act of Christ the Bridegroom towards the
Church the Bride. This is clear and unambiguous
when the sacramental ministry of the Eucharist, in
which the priest acts *in persona Christi*, is performed by
a man. (*Mulieris* §26)

Theologians have been genuinely appalled by John
Paul II's reflections. There is no need for me to discuss
this further. His audacious statement has not been
repeated by either Pope Benedict XVI or Pope Francis.

**No 4. *Ordinatio Sacerdotalis* ("Priestly Ordination") –
May 22, 1994.** Apostolic Letter by Pope John Paul II on
"Reserving Priestly Ordination to Men Alone."

The overall purpose of this document is to reiterate
Rome's official position against women's ordination.
After repeating the assertion that it was Jesus himself
who permanently excluded women from Holy Orders
and that this doctrine has been faithfully held on to in
the Church's Tradition, Pope John Paul II makes an
alarmingly authoritative declaration:

"In order that all doubt may be removed regarding
a matter of great importance, a matter which pertains
to the Church's divine constitution itself, in virtue of
my ministry of confirming the brethren (cf. *Lk* 22:32)

I declare that the Church has no authority whatsoever to confer priestly ordination on women and that this judgment is to be *definitively* held by all the Church's faithful." (§ 4)

No 5. *Responsum ad Dubium* ("Reply to a Doubt") – October 28, 1995. Declaration by the Congregation for the Doctrine of the Faith.

In this document, the Congregation for the Doctrine of Faith declares that the Church's inability to ordain women is "to be held always, everywhere, and by all, as *belonging to the deposit of the faith.*" An accompanying letter states that Pope John Paul II's decision was "an act of the ordinary papal magisterium, in itself not infallible, which witnesses to the infallibility of the teaching of a doctrine already possessed by the Church."

No 6. *Ad Tuendam Fidem* ("To Protect Faith") – May 28, 1998. An edict by Pope John Paul II by which certain norms are inserted into the Code of Canon Law.

No 7. Commentary on *Ad Tuendam Fidem* – June 29, 1998. Letter by Joseph Cardinal Ratzinger, Prefect of the Congregation for the Doctrine of the Faith.

Ad Tuendam Fidem updates church law regarding the Profession of Faith. Canon 750.2 now states that "everything set forth definitively by the Magisterium of the Church regarding teaching on faith and morals must be firmly accepted and held." In the accompanying commentary Cardinal Ratzinger explains this also refers to "the doctrine that priestly ordination is reserved only to men." Everyone who denies it "rejects a truth of Catholic doctrine and is therefore no longer in full communion with the Catholic Church."

**No 8.   The secret examination of new Bishops –
November 2, 2002.**

Among the list of secret questions to scrutinise
candidates for episcopacy, we find: "What does the
candidate think about women's ordination?"

**No 9. Decree by the Congregation for the Doctrine of
the Faith – May 30, 2008.**

"He who has attempted to confer Holy Orders on a
woman, and the woman who has attempted to receive
the said sacrament, incurs automatic excommunication,
reserved to the Apostolic See."

The full texts of all these documents can be found
online.

Appendix 2

Timeline

Some key dates in the worldwide movement toward
women in the diaconate and the priesthood

1944   Florence Li Tim Oi ordained "on an emergency
        basis" in Anglican Church in Hong Kong.

1947   First women ordained in Czechoslovak Hussite
        Church

1948   First women ordained in Evangelical Lutheran
        Church of Denmark

1949   First women ordained in Old Catholic Church
        (USA)

1956   First women ordained in Presbyterian Church (USA)

1962   **Opening of the Second Vatican Council to reform**
        the Catholic Church (Pope John XXIII)

1964   General Convention of Episcopal Church in USA
        changes deaconess canon to read "ordered" rather
        than "appointed."

1965   **Close of the Second Vatican Council (Pope Paul VI)**

1965   Deaconess Phyllis Edwards recognized as deacon by
        San Francisco Bishop James Pike of the Episcopal
        Church in USA.

1966   Episcopal Church Committee reports to the House
        of Bishops: *The Proper Place of Women in the Ministry of*
        the Church.

1966   Church of England publishes *Women and Holy Orders.*

1968   Church of England Working Party produces *Women in Ministry: a Study.*

1968   Lambeth Conference of the Anglican Church agrees that deaconesses are within the diaconate, but refers the ordination of women back to member churches for further study. Hong Kong, Kenya, Korea and Canada begin ordaining women to diaconate.

1969   Special General Convention of the Episcopal Church USA (at South Bend) changes canon so that women may be licensed to be lay readers and to administer the chalice.

1970   *What is ordination coming to?* Report of a Consultation on the Ordination of Women (World Council of Churches).

1970   Report on Ordination of Women in the American Lutheran Church

1970   Report of the Joint Commission on Ordained and Licensed Ministries in the Episcopal Church USA; report rejected by a narrow margin in the clergy order of the House of Deputies.

1970   At General Convention of the Episcopal Church USA: Women admitted as lay deputies after 50-year struggle. Women included in canon on deacons, eligible for Clergy Pension Fund; authorization for ordination of women to priesthood approved by laity but narrowly defeated by clerical deputies.

1971   Anglican Consultative Council (world Anglican body of clergy and laity meeting between Lambeth Conferences) declares it is "acceptable" for a bishop to ordain a woman if his national church or province approves.

1971 **During the Bishops' Synod in Rome, in the pontificate of Pope Paul VI, Cardinal Flahiff and the Canadian Bishops Conference ask for a study on women's ministries.**

1971 The Revs. Jane Hwang and Joyce Bennett are ordained to the priesthood in the Anglican Church by Bishop Gilbert Baker of Hong Kong; Florence Li Tim-Oi's orders are recognized in absentia.

1971 House of Bishops in Episcopal Church USA refers women's ordination for further study. Episcopal women begin to be ordained deacon alongside men.

1973 General Convention of Episcopal Church USA rejects ordination of women to priesthood.

Women deacons presented alongside men for ordination to priesthood in New York, but bishop refuses.

1973 American Lutheran Church releases report: *Can Women Serve in the Ordained Ministry?*

1973 **Pope Paul VI appoints a Special Commission on "the Function of Women in Society and in the Church" (FWSC). During meetings of the FWSC, a group of women members protests about lack of freedom of expression: "Our views are being systematically suppressed."**

1974 July 29: In Episcopal Church USA, eleven women deacons are ordained to priesthood by two retired and one resigned bishop in Philadelphia.

July 30: Some Episcopal women priests inhibited by their bishops from priestly functions, some from deacon's service; others agree voluntarily to refrain from priestly ministry.

July 31: Presiding Episcopal Bishop John Allin calls emergency meeting of House of Bishops.

Aug. 15: Episcopal bishops meet in Chicago and decry four bishops' "violation of collegiality," refuse to talk with women, and assert the ordinations were not valid. Women reject bishops' action; Charles Willie resigns as vice president of House of Deputies in protest. Ecclesiastical charges are filed against the Philadelphia bishops.

Oct. 18: House of Bishops reaffirms endorsement of ordaining women but votes almost unanimously not to act until General Convention approves.

Oct. 27: The Revs. Alison Cheek, Carter Heyward and Jeannette Piccard publicly celebrate an Episcopal Eucharist at New York City's Riverside Church.

1975   **Under Pope Paul VI, the Pontifical Biblical Commission reports that there are no scriptural objections to ordaining women to the Catholic priesthood. The Vatican suppresses the report, but its contents are leaked and become known.**

1975   Joint Study, *Pro & Con on Ordination of Women*, issued by the U.S. Anglican-Roman Catholic consultation in Cincinnati.

1975   John Wijngaards submits recommendation to the Indian Bishops' Conference: *The Ministry of Women and Social Myth.*

1975   Letter of Donald Coggan, Archbishop of Canterbury, Church of England, to Pope Paul VI

1975   A Working Group on the Ordination of Women
        set up by ARCIC (the Anglican/Roman Catholic
        International Consultation) meets in Assisi
        November 10-14, 1975. The two Roman Catholic
        theologians appointed by the Vatican, Frs. Hervé
        Legrand and Eric Doyle, both express support for
        the ordination of women. The report is suppressed
        by the Vatican under Pope Paul VI, but published
        by ARCIC.

1975   Letter of Pope Paul VI to Donald Coggan,
        Archbishop of Canterbury, Churh of England,
        asserting the Catholic stance against the ordination
        of women (November 30, 1975)

1976   Letter of Donald Coggan, Archbishop of Canterbury,
        to Pope Paul VI with another response from Pope
        Paul VI

1976   Pope Paul VI publishes *Inter Insigniores ("Among
        the Most Prominent")*, Declaration of the Sacred
        Congregation for the Doctrine of the Faith on
        the question of the admission of women to the
        ministerial priesthood.

1977   Commentary by the Sacred Congregation for
        the Doctrine of the Faith on Pope Paul VI's
        declaration, *Inter Insigniores*

1977   Anglican Church of Canada begins ordaining women.

1977   Women ordained in Philadelphia and Washington
        in Episcopal Church USA begin to be "regularized,"
        and regular ordinations of women to the priesthood
        begin with 100 ordained by year's end.

1977   Anglican Church in New Zealand begins ordaining
        women to the priesthood.

1981   Women accepted as deacons in Church of England

1983   **New Code of Church Law: the exclusion of women from ordination again entered into law, under Pope John Paul II.**

1984   **Letter of Pope John Paul II to Robert Runcie, Archbishop of Canterbury**

1985   Church of England in the UK decides to ordain women as deacons.

1985   Letter of Robert Runcie, Archbishop of Canterbury, Church of England, to Pope John Paul II

1985   Letter of Robert Runcie, Archbishop of Canterbury, to Cardinal Jan Willebrands, President of the Vatican Secretariat for Promoting Christian Unity

1986   **Letter of Cardinal Jan Willebrands, President of the Vatican Secretariat for Promoting Christian Unity, to Robert Runcie, Archbishop of Canterbury**

1987   UK synod votes in favor of women's ordination in Church of England.

1988   The final plan for women's ordination in the Church of England was submitted in June. It passed the Synod in July and the House of Bishops in August.

1988   **Women's participation in the life and mission of the Church described in *Christifideles Laici* ("Christian lay faithful") by Pope John Paul II.**

1988   First woman bishop elected in Episcopal Church of the USA.

1988   **Pope John Paul II publishes *Mulieris Dignitatem,* "On the Dignity and Vocation of Women."**

1994   Pope John Paul II publishes *Ordinatio Sacerdotalis*, apostolic letter on Reserving Priestly Ordination to Men Alone.

1994   *New Catechism of the Catholic Church* asserts women's exclusion from ordination.

1995   Pope John Paul II issues *Letter to Women*, in preparation for the Fourth World Conference on Women, in Beijing.

1995   Pope John Paul II issues *Responsum ad Dubium* ("Response to a Doubt"), reaffirming the teaching contained in *Ordinatio Sacerdotalis*.

1998   Pope John Paul II issues *Ad Tuendam Fidem* ("To Protect Faith"), declaring the exclusion of women is "definitive" doctrine.

1998   Commentary on *Ad Tuendam Fidem* contains the judgment that those who hold that women can be ordained priests are "no longer in full communion with the Catholic Church." This was written by Cardinal Joseph Ratzinger, Secretary of the Sacred Congregation for the Doctrine of the Faith.

1998   Belgian Bishops' Conference: Commission on "Woman and the Church," in report *Who May Dwell Within your Tent?* leaves room for legitimate dissent in the Church.

1998   John Wijngaards issues press release, also published in the *Times* of London: "Why I resigned from the priestly ministry."

1999   Academic website launched: www.womenpriests.org.

2001   First international conference of Catholic Women's Ordination Worldwide, held in Dublin.

2001   John Wijngaards publishes *The Ordination of Women in the Catholic Church.*

2002   John Wijngaards publishes *No Women in Holy Orders? The Ancient Women Deacons.*

2015   The Wijngaards Institute submits a *Documented Appeal to Pope Francis* to request the re-instatement of the ordained diaconate for women; the appeal is co-signed by 20 major international Catholic organizations.

2016   Pope Francis establishes the *Study Commission on the Women's Diaconate.*

Appendix 3

The genetic basis of gender roles

Some people are so fanatical about equality of rights that they seem anxious to minimise the differences between the sexes at all costs. Unisex clothing and trans-sexual hairstyles witness to a similar tendency. It is doubtful whether a society with more masculine women and more feminine men will be a happier community in which to live. What's more, the notion seems doomed to failure.

Men and women are different, both biologically and psychologically. There are inborn traits which predispose them to different tasks in the family. Although such differences should not be exaggerated, they are part and parcel of a person's physical and mental make-up.

Man's body is much better adapted to rough physical work. In the way man's physique is built, his central and massive "body-ness" is formed by the chest. Man has broad shoulders and strong arms. Man has much stronger muscles than woman, and this is borne out by international sports achievements. In short, man projects an image of physical strength.

Woman, on the other hand, possesses a body that is structured for motherhood. For her the central "body-ness" is constituted by the womb. The physique of woman is "more gracious," obviously evolved in this way to attract the partner by her beauty and to protect the offspring by her reserves in natural energy. It stands to reason that the physical and psychological implications of motherhood dispose the woman to perform certain roles in family and in society rather than other ones.

Nor is it just a matter of physique. Men and women start life with a different emotional disposition, as has been proved by psychologists in various tests. Before boys and girls can have been influenced by prejudices of the culture to which they belong, they already show different attitudes to their environment. Generally speaking, boys play more roughly, show more aggression, are more inclined to be obstinate, and are more easily given to violence. Girls yield more easily and are more affectionate. These findings have been confirmed by studies in different social milieus and cultures. Already in the first three years of life males seem to be more aggressive, females more nurturing in their approach.

Studies of the human brain show marked differences between the brains of men and women. A man's mind is more geared to perform spatial tasks and mathematics. A woman's mind seems structured to cope better with interactive skills. Neuroscientists have documented gender differences in many brain functions; for instance, in navigation, working memory, defensiveness, empathy and self-regulation.

The different dispositions of men and women to aggressive and nurturing tasks seem to be related to, if not the result of, different hormone activity in the body. The massive increase of the androgen hormone in boys at puberty (from 10 to 30 times the previous level) is related to increased aggressiveness of the young adolescent.

The innate differences can also be proved to some

extent by the actual division of labour in society. In practically all primitive societies, aggressive jobs were done by men. It is the men who did the hunting, fishing, metalworking, weapon making, boat building and so on. The women usually ground corn, gathered fruit and seeds, made and repaired clothes, and did the housework. Although part of this may have been culture-determined, the fact that the same division of labour was followed in 224 economically primitive societies from all over the world shows that it must have been partly based on the biological makeup of men and women.

However, differences in a woman's physical or mental gifts do not make her inferior or incapable of leadership – contrary to what many in the Church hierarchy maintained for centuries.

Sources

Primary and historical sources

Abbott, Walter (ed.). *The Documents of Vatican II*. New York: America Press, 1966.

Aquinas, Thomas. *Summa Theologica*. English translation, London: Burns and Oates, 1922.

Badini Confalonieri, Luca. *Democracy in the Christian Church. An Historical, Theological and Political Case*. London: Bloomsbury T&T Clark, 2012.

Bonaventure. *Omnia Opera*. Rome: Quaracchi, 1889.

Catechism of the Catholic Church. London: Continuum, 2000.

Codex Iuris Canonici. The Code of Canon Law promulgated by Pope Benedict XV. Freiburg: Herder, 1918.

Denzinger, Heinrich (ed.). *Enchiridion Symbolorum*. Freibourg: Herder, 1955.

Eliade, Mircea. *Traité d'Histoire des Réligions*. Paris: Payot, 1959.

Flannery, Austin (ed.). *Vatican Council II*. New York: Costello, 1988.

Friedberg, Emil (ed.). *Corpus Juris Canonici*, Leipzig 1879-1881; reprint Graz: Akademische Druck- u. Verlagsanstalt, 1955.

Gaillardetz, Richard. *Teaching with Authority. A Theology of the Magisterium in the Church*, Liturgical Press, Collegeville 1997.

Jerusalem Bible. Complete translation of Sacred Scripture. London: Darton, Longman & Todd, 1966.

Kateusz, Ally. *Mary and Early Christian Women: Hidden Leadership*. Cham: Palgrave Macmillan, 2019.

LaPorte, Jean. *The Role of Women in Early Christianity*. New York:

Edwin Mellen Press, 1982.

Macy, Gary. *The Hidden History of Women's Ordination: Female Clergy In The Medieval West.* Oxford: University Press, 2008.

Migne, Jacques Paul (ed.). *Patrologia Graeca.* Paris: Imprimerie Catholique, 1857-1866.

Migne, Jacques Paul (ed.). *Patrologia Latina.* Paris: Imprimerie Catholique, 1841-1855.

Newman, John Henry. *Conscience, Consensus and the Development of Doctrine: Revolutionary Texts.* James Gaffney (ed.), Image/ Doubleday, New York 1992.

Rahner, Karl (ed.). *Sacramentum Mundi.* London: Herder, 1969.

Papal documents pertaining to women's ordination (chronological order)

Inter Insigniores ('Among the Most Significant') - 15 October 1976. 'Declaration of the Sacred Congregation for the Doctrine of the Faith on the question of the admission of women to the ministerial priesthood', *Acta Apostolicae Sedis 55* (1963) pp. 267-268; *Briefing 7* (1977) no. 5 & 6.

Commentary on 'Inter Insigniores' (27 January 1977). Commentary by the Sacred Congregation for the Doctrine of the Faith, *Acta Apostolicae Sedis* 69 (1977) pp. 98-116; *L'Osservatore Romano,* Thursday 27 January 1977.

Mulieris Dignitatem ('Women's Dignity') - 15 August 1988. Apostolic Letter of Pope John Paul II on the Dignity and Vocation of Women, no. 26; *Acta Apostolicae Sedis* 80 (1988) p. 1715; Pauline Books, Boston, 1999.

Donum Veritatis ('The Gift of Truth') - 24 May 1990. Instruction on the Ecclesial Vocation of the Theologian by the Congregation for the Doctrine of the Faith, *Acta Apostolicae Sedis* 82 (1990) pp. 1550-1570; *Origins* 20 (1990) 5 July.

Ordinatio Sacerdotalis ('Priestly Ordination') - 22 May 1994.
Apostolic Letter by Pope John Paul II on Reserving Priestly
Ordination to Men Alone, *Origins* 24 (1994) June 9;
L'Osservatore Romano 24 November 1994.

Responsum ad Dubium ('Reply to a Doubt') 28 October 1995.
Declaration by the Congregation for the Doctrine of the
Faith, *Origins* 25 (1995) November 30.

Ad Tuendam Fidem ('To Protect Faith') - May 28, 1998. *Motu
Proprio* by Pope John Paul II by which certain norms are
inserted into the Code of Canon Law, *L'Osservatore Romano* 15
July 1998; *Origins* 28 (1998) 16 July.

Commentary on Ad Tuendam Fidem (29 June 1998). Commentary
by Joseph Cardinal Ratzinger, Prefect of the Congregation for
the Doctrine of the Faith, *L'Osservatore Romano* 15 July 1998.

Books and articles focusing on the priestly ordination of women

Ackermann, Denise. 'Feminist Liberation Theology. A
Contextual Option', *Journal of Theology for Southern Africa*, 62
(1988) pp. 14-18.

Aubert, Jean-Marie. 'Women Priests?' in *La femme: antiféminisme
et christianisme*. Paris: Cerf-Desclée, 1975; online http://www.
womenpriests.org/theology/aubert.asp.

Avis, Paul (ed.). *Seeking the Truth of Change in the Church:
Reception, Communion and the Ordination of Women*. London:
Mowbrays, 2004.

Azkoul, Michael. *Order of Creation. Order of Redemption*.
Rollinsford: Orthodox Research Institute, 2007.

Beattie, Tina. 'Mary, the Virgin Priest?' *The Month*, 257 (1996)
pp. 485-493.

Beattie, Tina. *God's Mother, Eve's Advocate. A Gynocentric
Refiguration of Marian Symbolism*. Bristol: Centre for

Comparative Studies, 1999.

Begley-Armbruster, John. 'Women and Office in the Church,' *American Ecclesiastical Review* 165 (1971) pp. 145-57.

Black, Patricia. 'The New is Elsewhere': Women's Leadership in Community-Profit Organisations. Brisbane: Queensland University of Technology, 1999.

Børresen, Kari Elisabeth. 'The Ordination of Women: to Nurture Tradition by Continuing Inculturation', *Studia Theologica* 46 (1992) pp. 3-13.

Bouyer, Louis. *Woman in the Church*. San Francisco: Ignatius Press, 1979.

Bowman, Ann, 'Women in Ministry: An Exegetical Study of I Timothy 2:11-15': *Biblical Studies* 149 (1992) 193-213.

Brady, Veronica. 'The God of Small Things: God, Women and the Question of Power', *Basic Newsletter* 4 (2000) pp. 20-27.

Broome, Catharina. 'The Priestly Vocation of Thérèse of the Child of Jesus', *Spirituality* (1997) pp. 225-230.

Brown Zikmund, Barbara et al. *Clergy Women: An Uphill Calling*. Westminster: AbeBooks, 1998.

Burns, Peter. 'Women's Ordination and Infallible Teaching, an Inquiry'. *Basic Newsletter* 1 (1997) pp. 1-12.

Byrne, Lavinia. *On Being Woman in the Church*. London: SPCK, 1998.

Byrne, Lavinia. *Woman At The Altar: The Ordination of Women in the Roman Catholic Church*. New York: Continuum, 1999.

Carr, Anne. 'Is a Christian Feminist Theology Possible?', *Theological Studies* 43 (1982) pp. 279-297.

Carroll, Elizabeth. 'Women and Ministry', *Theological Studies* 36 (1975) pp. 660-687.

Casey, Damien. 'The "Fractio Panis" and the Eucharist as

Eschatological Banquet – implications for women's ministry', *Mcauley University Electronic Journal*, 18 August 2002.

Chenderlin, Francis, 'Women as ordained priests? Should women be allowed to consecrate?', *Homeletic and Pastoral Review* 72 (1972) no. 8, pp. 25-32; 'Women priests - more thoughts but no second thoughts,' ib. 73 (1973) no. 5, pp. 13-22.

Chittister, Joan. *Winds of Change: Women Challenge the Church*. Kansas City: Sheed & Ward, 1986.

Clark, Stephen. *Man and Woman in Christ*. Ann Arbor: Servant Publications, 1980.

Coffey, David. 'Priestly Representation and Women's Ordination', in *Priesthood: The Hard Questions*, Gerald Gleeson (ed.), Dublin 1993, pp. 79-99.

Coriden, James (ed.). *Sexism and Church Law: Equal Rights and Affirmative Action*. New York: Paulist Press, 1977.

Cypser, Cora. *Taking off the Patriarchal Glasses*. Katonah: Kim Pathways, 1987.

Daniélou, Jean. *The Ministry of Women in the Early Church*. Leighton Buzzard: Faith Press, 1974.

Donovan, Mary. *Women Priests in the Episcopal Church: The Experience of the First Decade*. Cincinnati: Forward Movement Publications, 1988.

Doyle, Eric. 'The Question of Women Priests and the Argument "in Persona Christi"', *Irish Theological Quarterly* 50 (1983-1984) pp. 212-221.

Ferder, Fran. *Called to Break Bread?* Mount Rainer: Quixote Centre, 1978.

Fitzmyer, Joseph. 'Fidelity to Jesus and the ordination of women', *America* 175 (1996) pp. 9-12.

Ford, John M. 'Biblical Material relevant to the Ordination of

Women,' *Journal of Ecumenical Studies* 10 (1973), pp. 669-94.

France, Richard. *Women in the Church's Ministry: A Test Case for Biblical Interpretation*. Grand Rapids: Eerdmans, 1997.

Furlong, Monica (ed.). *Feminine in the Church*. London: SPCK, 1984.

Gaillardetz, Richard. 'Infallibility and the Ordination of Women. A Note on the CDF *Responsum ad Dubium* regarding the Authoritative Status of *Ordinatio Sacerdotalis*', *Louvain Studies* 21 (1996) pp. 3-24.

Gardiner, Anne Marie (ed.). *Women and the Catholic Church*. New York: Paulist Press, 1976.

Gebara, Ivonne. *Longing for Running Water: Ecofeminism and Liberation*. Minneapolis: Fortress Press, 1999.

Goddard, Lis et. al. *AWESOME Voices: God working through ordained women today*. Malton: Gilead Books, 2019.

Gould, Graham. *God's Work of Art: Essays Celebrating the Tenth Anniversary of the Ordination of Women to the Priesthood in the Church*. London: Watch, 2004.

Grant, Jacquelyn. *White Women's Christ and Black Women's Jesus: Feminist Christology and Womanist Response*. Atlanta: Scholars Press, 1989.

Green, Ali. *A Theology of Women's Priesthood*. London: SPCK, 2009.

Greenacre, Roger & Podmore, Colin. *Part of the One Church?: The Ordination of Women and Anglican Identity*. Canterbury Press, 2014.

Greshake, Gisbert. 'Response to the Declaration of the Congregation for Doctrine regarding the doctrine proposed in the apostolic letter *Ordinatio Sacerdotalis*', *Pastoralblatt* 48 (1996) 56-57.

Grey, Mary. *Redeeming the Dream: Feminism, Redemption and*

Christian Tradition. London: SPCK, 1989.

Hamilton, Michael and Montgomery, Nancy (eds.). *The Ordination of Women: Pro and Con*. New York: Morehouse Barlow, 1975.

Häring, Hermann. 'The Authority of Women and the Future of the Church', *Concilium* 38/3 (June 1999) pp. 117-125.

Hannon, V. Emmanuel. *The Question of Women in Priesthood*. London: Geoffrey Chapman, 1967.

Hauke, Manfred. *Women in the Priesthood? A Systematic Analysis in the Light of the Order of Creation and Redemption*. San Francisco: Ignatius Press, 1992.

Heinzelmann, Gertrud (ed.). *We Won't Keep Silence Any Longer!* Zürich: Interfeminas Verlag, 1964.

Heyer, Robert (ed.). *Women and Orders*. New York: Paulist Press, 1974.

Hopko, Thomas (ed.). *Women and the Priesthood*. Crestwood, NY: St. Vladimir's Seminary Press, 1983.

Hugenberger, Gordon. 'Women in Church Office: Hermeneutics or Exegesis? A Survey of Approaches to I Timothy 2:8-15', *Journal of the Evangelical Theological Society* 35 (1992) 341-360.

Irvin, Dorothy. 'The Ministry of Women in the Early Church: The Archeological Evidence', *Duke Divinity School Review* 2 (1980) pp. 76-86.

Jensen, Anne. 'The Representation of Christ, Ecclesiastical Office, and Presiding at the Eucharist', *Freiburger Zeitschrift für Philosophie und Theologie* 40 (1993) pp. 282-297.

Jensen, Anne. *God's Self-Confident Daughters: Early Christianity and the Liberation of Women*. Louisville: John Knox Press, 1996.

Johnson, Elizabeth. 'Disputed questions: authority, priesthood, women', *Commonweal*, vol. 123, January 26, 1996, pp. 8-10.

Johnson, Elizabeth. *She Who Is: The Mystery of God in Feminist Theological Discourse*. New York: Crossroad, 1992.

Jones, Ian et al. *Women and Ordination in the Christian Churches: International Perspectives*. London: T & T Clark, 2008.

Kilmartin, Edward. 'Apostolic Office: Sacrament of Christ', *Theological Studies* 36 (1975) pp. 243-264.

Kirk, Geoffrey. *Without Precedent: Scripture, Tradition, and the Ordination of Women*. Eugene: Wipf & Stock, 2016.

Komonchak, Joseph. 'Theological Questions on the Ordination of Women'. *Report on Women's Ordination Conference*, Detroit 1976, Appendix E.

Knoll, Benjamin & Bolin, Cammie. *She Preached the Word: Women's Ordination in Modern America*. Oxford: University Press, 2018.

Lakeland, Paul. *Can Women be Priests?* Dublin: Mercier Press, 1975.

Legrand, Hervé. 'Views on the Ordination of Women,' *Origins*, Jan. 6, 1977; reprinted in *Briefing* 7 (1977), no. 6, pp. 22-35.

Legrand, Hervé. 'The Non-ordination of Women: Tradition or Simply an Historical Fact?', *Worship* 65 (1991) pp. 482-508.

Macy, Gary. 'The Ordination of Women in the Early Middle Ages'. *Theological Studies* 61 (2000) pp. 481-507.

Manning, Joanna. *Is the Pope Catholic? A Woman Confronts her Church*. Toronto: Malcolm Lester, 1999.

McAleese, Mary. 'Coping with a Christ who does not want women priests almost as much as He wants Ulster to remain British'. In *Women Sharing Fully*, BASIC Seminar, Dublin, 1995, pp. 11-21.

McEwan, Dorothea. 'The Ordination of Women – A Living Tradition'. In *Pogranicza Wrazliwosci w Literaturze i Kulturze*, Szczecin, Poland, 2-4 June 1997.

Meyer, Edward. 'Are there theological reasons why the church should not ordain women priests?', *Review for Religious* 34 (1975/76), pp. 957-67.

Micks, Marianne and Price, Charles (eds.). *Towards a New Theology of Ordination: Essays on the Ordination of Women.* Somerville: Greeno, Hadden & Company, 1976.

Milhaven, Annie. 'The Real Reasons Why the Catholic Church Does Not Ordain Women', *Conscience* 18 (1997) no. 3, pp. 12-14.

Montefiori, Hugh (ed.). *Yes to Women Priests.* Southend-on-Sea: Mayhew McCrimmon, 1978.

Moore, Peter (ed.). *Man, Woman and Priesthood.* London: SPCK, 1979.

Morris, Joan. *Against Nature and God: The History of Women with Clerical Ordination and the Jurisdiction of Bishops.* London: Mowbrays, 1973.

Nadell, Pamela. *Women Who Would be Rabbis: A History of Women's Ordination, 1889-1985.* Boston: Beacon Press, 1999.

National Assembly of Women Religious. *Women in Ministry: A Sisters' View.* Chicago, 1972.

Nientiedt, Klaus. 'How Binding? "Ordinatio Sacerdotalis" unleashes debate on the Magisterium', *Herder Korrespondenz* 9 (1996) pp. 461-466.

O'Hara Graff, Ann. 'Infallibility complex: Have we heard the final word on women's ordination?', *U.S. Catholic*, vol. 61, April 1996, pp. 6-11.

Otranto, Giorgio. 'Notes on the Female Priesthood in Antiquity', *Journal of Feminist Studies* 7 (1991) pp. 73 – 94.

Poole, Myra & Bonner, Pippa. *Awakening - Catholic Women's Ordination From The Public Square.* London: Fisher King, 2015.

Raab, Kelley. *When Women Become Priests.* New York: Columbia

University Press, 2000.

Raming, Ida. *The Exclusion of Women from the Priesthood: Divine Law or Sex Discrimination?* Metuchen: Scarecrow Press, 1976.

Raming, Ida. *A History of Women and Ordination.* Toronto: Scarecrow Press, 2004.

Rhodes, Lynn. *Co-Creating. A Feminist Vision of Ministry.* Philadelphia: John Knox Press, 1987.

Rosenblatt, Marie-Eloise (ed.). *Where can we find her? Searching for women's identity in the new church.* Mahwah: Paulist Press, 1991.

Russell, Lettie M. *Church in the Round: Feminist Interpretation of the Church.* Louisville: John Knox Press, 1993.

Ruether, Rosemary. *The Role of Women in Society and in the Church.* Ottawa: Canadian Religious Conference, 1975.

Ruether, Rosemary and McLaughlin, Eleanor. *Women of Spirit: Female Leadership in the Jewish and Christian Traditions.* New York: Simon & Schuster, 1978.

Schüssler Fiorenza, Elisabeth. *In Memory of Her: Feminist Theological Reconstruction of Christian Origins.* New York: Herder & Herder, 1983.

Soskice, Janet (ed.). *After Eve: Women, Theology and the Christian Tradition.* London: Collins Marshall Pickering, 1990.

Storkey, Elaine. *Women and the Church: What's Right with Feminism.* London: SPCK, 1985.

Strachan, Elspeth and Gordon. *Freeing the Feminine.* Dunbar: Labarum Publications, 1985.

Stuhlmueller, Carroll (ed.). *Women and Priesthood: Future Directions.* Collegeville: Liturgical Press, 1978.

Sweeley, John. *The Validity of Women's Ordination to the Roman Catholic Priesthood: Catholicism for the Twenty-First Century.* Ohio: St James Press, 2018.

Swidler, Arlene & Leonard. *Women Priests*. New York: Paulist Press, 1977.

Taddei-Ferretti, Cloe. *Even the Dogs: The Ordination of Women in the Catholic Church*. London: LIT Verlag, 2017.

Tavard, George. *Woman in Christian Tradition*. Notre Dame University Press, 1973.

Thompsett, Frederica. *Looking Forward, Looking Backward: Forty Years of Women's Ordination*. New York: Morehouse, 2014.

Terwilliger, Robert and Holmes, Urban (eds.). *To be a priest: Perspectives on Vocation and Ordination*. New York: Seabury Press, 1975.

Tetlow, Elisabeth. *Women and Ministry in the New Testament*. New York: Paulist Press, 1985.

Torjesen, Karen Jo. *When Women Were Priests*. New York: HarperOne, 1993.

Van der Meer, Haye. *Women Priests in the Catholic Church?* Philadelphia: Temple University Press, 1973.

Van Eyden, René. 'Women Ministers in the Catholic Church?', *Sisters Today* 40 (1968) pp. 211-226.

Van Eyden, René. 'The Creation of Womanhood: A Hierarchical Construction'. From *Olhares feministas sobre a Igreja Católica*. São Paulo: Publicações CDD, 2001.

Von Hildebrand, Alice and Kreeft, Peter. *Women and the Priesthood*. Steubenville: Franciscan University Press, 1994.

Vyhmeister, Nancy (ed.). *Women in Ministry*. Berrien Springs: Andrews University 1998.

Wakeman, Hilary (ed.). *Women Priests: The First Years*. London: Darton. Longman & Todd, 1996.

Walrond-Skinner, Sue (ed.). *Crossing the Boundary: What Will Women Priests Mean?* London: Bloomsbury Publishing, 1994.

Ware, Kallistos. 'Man, Woman and the Priesthood of Christ,' in *Women and the Priesthood*, ed. Thomas Hopko. Crestwood, NY: St. Vladimir's Seminary Press, 1983, pp. 9-37.

Wiklander, Bertil. *Ordination Reconsidered: The Biblical Vision of Men and Women as Servants of God*. Bracknell: Newbold Academic Press, 2015.

Wilson, Harold (ed.). *Women Priests? Yes – Now!* Denham: Denham House Press, 1975.

Wijngaards, John. 'The Ministry of Women and Social Myth,' in *Ministries in the Church in India*, ed. D. S. Amalorpavadas, New Delhi, 1976, pp. 221-250.

Wijngaards, John. *Did Christ Rule Out Women Priests?* McCrimmons, Great Wakering 1977 (2nd edition in 1986).

Wijngaards, John. *The Ordination of Women in the Catholic Church: Unmasking a Cuckoo's Egg Tradition*. London: Darton, Longman & Todd, 2001; New York: Continuum, 2001.

Wijngaards, John. 'Are women substantially incompatible for the priesthood?', *National Catholic Reporter*, 18 June 2018.

References

p. x – *...because he is with you, he is in you.*: John 14,16-17. In the original Greek the Spirit is neutral (pneuma). In English I translate the Spirit as a 'he' rather than an impersonal 'it'.

p. x – *...as a teacher, an interpreter.*: H. Schlier, 'The Holy Spirit as interpreter according to St. John's Gospel', *Communio* 1 (1974) 128141; G. Johnston, 'The Spirit-Paraclete in the Gospel of John', Perspective 9 (1968) 29-37; H.F. Woodhouse, 'The Interpreter', *Biblical Theology* 18 (1968) 51-53; J. Wijngaards, *The Spirit in John*, Michael Glazier, Wilmington 1988, pp. 49-78.

p. x – *...everything I have said to you.*: John 14, 25-26.

p. xi – *...things that lie in the future.*: John 16, 12-14.

p. 26 – *...at the opportune moment.*: Flannery, Austin (ed.), *Vatican Council II*, Vol. 1, Costello, New York, 1988, p. 459.

Chapter 1. The discovery and the shock

p. 33 – *...for theological study.*: The sisters were sent to the Regina Mundi College for Women.

p. 36 – *"The law of the Church forbids it!"*: The Code of Canon Law promulgated by Pope Benedict XV in 1917 still prescribed that only male clerics could touch, wash and maintain chalices, patens, purificators, palls and corporals. *Codex Iuris Canonici*, ed. Herder, Freiburg 1918, canon 1306, § 1-2.

Chapter 2. The truth comes clearer

p. 41 – *...we are speaking about.*: The text was published as 'The Ministry of Women and Social Myth', in *New Ministries in*

India', D. S. Amalopavadass (ed.), NBCLC, Bangalore 1976, pp. 50-80.

p. 42 – *...women from Holy Orders.*: The report was said to have been leaked to the media by its chairman, David Stanley, SJ. See *Women Priests*, Arlene Swidler & Leonard Swidler (eds.), Paulist Press 1977, pp. 338-346.

p. 42 – *...met in Assisi.*: Read the paper submitted by Eric Doyle, one of the Catholic representatives at the meeting; http://www.womenpriests.org/theology/doyle1.asp.

p. 42 – *...ordination of women.*: The correspondence between Rome and Canterbury can be found here: http://www.womenpriests.org/church/cant1.asp#coggan2.

p. 42 – *...women to the Ministerial Priesthood.*: *Women Priests*, Arlene Swidler & Leonard Swidler (eds.), Paulist Press 1977, pp. 37-49.

p. 43 – *...all the Church's faithful.*: '*Ordinatio Sacerdotalis*', *Origins* 24 (1994) June 9; *L'Osservatore Romano* 24 November 1994.

p. 43 – *...the Roman Pontiff.*: Papal Bull '*Unam Sanctam*' (One Holy Church), 18 November 1302, in Heinrich Denzinger, *Enchiridion Symbolorum*, Freiburg, Herder 1955, no. 468-469.

p. 43 – *...the Catholic Church.*: Papal Bull '*Cantate Domino*' (Sing to the Lord), 4 February 1442, Denzinger ib., no. 714.

p. 44 – *...the Lord Jesus Christ.*: Commentary on *Inter Insigniores* § 21, 40, 41.

Chapter 3. Cultural prejudice and social myth

p. 48 – *...made the caste system possible.*: Good background reading to the various implications of the term 'myth' used in this sense is provided by P. Maranda (Ed), *Mythology. Selected Readings*, Penguin 1972; see also Sh. Hincliff & M. Gott, 'Challenging Social Myths and Stereotypes of Women and Aging', *Journal of Women & Aging* 20 (2008) pp. 65-81.

p. 49 – "...*the female is ruled.*": Aristotle, *Generation of Animals* I 82f, 728a; *Politica*, 1254 b 10-14; C. Whitbeck, 'Theories of Sex Difference', in Gould and Wartofsky (eds.), *Women and Philosophy*, New York 1976, pp. 54-80; M. Maloney, Ibid, 'The Arguments for Women's Difference in Classical Philosophy and Early Christianity', pp. 41-49; K. E. Power, 'Of godly men and medicine: ancient biology and the Christian Fathers on the nature of woman', *Woman-Church* 15 (1994) pp. 26-33.

p. 50 – ...*women remained the same.*: L. Wenger, *Institutes of the Roman Law of Civil Procedure*, Littleton 1940; F.Schulz, *Classical Roman Law*, London 1951; H. Heumann and E. Seckel, *Handlexikon zu den Quellen des römischen Rechts*, Graz 1958, pp. 246 and 265; M. Käser, *Roman Private Law*, Oxford 1965.

p. 51– ...*popes and bishops.*: *Decretum Gratiani* published in *Corpus Juris Canonici*, edited by A. Friedberg, Leipzig 1879-1881; reprint Graz 1955. See also I. Raming, *The Exclusion of Women from the Priesthood: Divine Law or Sex Discrimination?*, The Scarecrow Press, Metuchen, N.J. 1976.

p. 51 – ...*weakness of mind.*: *Decretum Gratiani* Causa 32, qu. 7, ch. 18.

p. 51 – ...*state of servitude.*: *Decretum Gratiani* Causa 33, qu. 5, ch. 11.

p. 51 – ...*image of God.*: *Decretum Gratiani* Causa 33, qu. 5, ch. 11, 13, 15 & 19.

p. 52 – ...*husbands by nature.*: *Decretum Gratiani* Causa 33, qu. 5, ch. 11, 13, 15 & 19.

p. 52 – ...*in the church.*: *Decretum Gratiani* Distinction 2 de cons., ch 29.

p. 52 – ...*priests or deacons.*: *Decretum Gratiani* Causa 2, question 7, princ.

p. 52 – ...*make the atmosphere humid....*: Aquinas, *Summa Theologica* I qu. 92, art 1, ad 1.

p. 53 – ...*just another accident....*: Aquinas, *De Veritate* 5, 9, d. 9.

p. 53 – ...*Aristotle had already pointed out.*: Aquinas, *Summa Theologica* I qu. 92, art 1, ad 1 & II, qu. 18, art. 1, ad 4.

p. 53 – ...*Women not so.*: Aquinas, *Summa Theologica* I qu. 92, art. 1.

p. 53 – ...*they resemble men.*: Aquinas, *Summa Theologica* I qu. 92, art. 2 & I qu. 93, art. 4 ad 1.

p. 53 – ...*naturally subject to men.*: Aquinas, *Summa Theologica* I qu. 92, art. 1, ad 2.

p. 53 – ...*the sacrament of Orders.*: Aquinas, *Summa Theologica* Suppl. qu. 39 art. 1.

p. 54 – ...*ample bibliography.*: *The Ordination of Women in the Catholic Church: Unmasking a Cuckoo's Egg Tradition*, Darton, Longman & Todd, London 2001; also published in the USA (Continuum 2001) and India (Media House 2002). Dutch edition: Narratio, Gorcum 2002; Italian: Meridiana, Molfetta 2002; Japanese: Akashi Shoten, Tokyo 2006; French: Chrétiens Autrement, Paris 2006.

p. 55 – ...*bear his sign.*: Bonaventure, *Commentarium in IV Libros Sententiarum Magistri Petri Lombardi* Div XXV, Art II, Qu I.

Chapter 4. Don't blame it on Jesus!

p. 57 – ...*Rome says.*: Inter Insigniores §9; Mulieris Dignitatem §26.

p. 59 – ...*human rights.*: O. Chadwick, *A History of Christianity*, Barnes & Noble, London 1995; J. Bronowski, *The Ascent of Man*, Angus & Robertson, Sydney 1973; Th. Safley, *The Reformation of Charity: The Secular and the Religious in Early Modern Poor Relief*, Brill, Boston 2003; Th. Woods Jr, *How the Catholic Church Built Western Civilization*, Regnery, Washington 2005; D. Gushee, *The Sacredness of Human Life: Why an Ancient Biblical Vision Is Key to the World's Future*, Eerdmans, Grand Rapids 2013; D. Kim & S. Kaul eds., *Imagining Human Rights*, de Gruyter, Berlin 2015.

p. 59 – ...*twelve had to be men.*: M. Karrer, "Apostle, Apostolate", in *The Encyclopedia of Christianity* Vol. 1, Eerdmans, Grand Rapids 1999, pp. 107-108.

p. 60 – *...decide about their future.*: Gen 43, 1-15; 2 Sam 13, 23-27

p. 60 – *...could a daughter inherit.*: Num 27, 1-11; 36, 1-12

p. 60 – *...distribute it to his sons.*: Dt 21, 15-17

p. 60 – *...Prodigal Son...*: Lk 15, 11-32

p. 60 – *...work by their father.*: Mt 21, 28-31

p. 60 – *...owner of the house...*: Lk 22, 11

p. 60 – *...builds the house...*: Mt 7, 24-27

p. 60 – *...defends it against intruders.*: Mt 12, 29

p. 60 – *...mentioning the queen.*: Mt 22, 1-14

p. 60 – *...friends of the bridegroom.*: Mt 9, 15

p. 62 – *...nor a staff!*: Mt 10, 9-10; Lk 10,4

p. 62 – *...ride on horseback.*: Mt 21, 1-7

p. 63 – *...cure the sick.*: Mk 3, 16; Mt 10, 1; Lk 9, 1

p. 64 – *...fill up the number.*: Acts 1, 15-26

p. 64 – *...passion and resurrection.*: Acts 1, 21-22

Chapter 5. Jesus' positive attitude toward women

p. 66 – *...business owners...*: Lydia of Thyatira; Acts 16, 14-15

p. 66 – *...administrators of property.*: Among them Doxa, Eupraxia, Anthousa and Irene; U. E. Eisen, *Amtsträgerinnen im frühen Christentum*, Göttingen 1996, pp. 210-213.

p. 66 – *...local magistrates.*: For instance Aurelia Hamasta and Memodora; J. Donaldson, *Woman: Her Position and Influence in Ancient Greece and Rome*, Kessinger reprint 2005, pp. 237-238.

p. 68 – *...when Christ was to come.*: 1 Thess 4, 15.

The same is implied in Paul's letter to the Corinthians of 57 A.D. The early Christians were quite time-conscious about the final salvation which Jesus' second coming would bring.

It is not difficult to see that such high-strung expectations had unbelievable consequences for the Christian's life. Some new converts at Thessalonica had stopped working altogether and were idly waiting for the last day. Paul disapproved of this and warned against exaggerated oracles foretelling the imminence of the Lord's Day. Some felt deceived and disappointed when Christ did not come as soon as they had anticipated.

Christians whose lives are dominated by the belief that the end of the world can come any day are no longer interested in building up their own world. They are literally like people looking up into the sky. They forget that they have a job to do on earth. Luke tried to correct such a mistaken attitude.

p. 68 – *...era of the Church.*: For a good background study of this theme of Luke's, see H. Conzelmann, *The Theology of Saint Luke*, Faber and Faber 1960.

p. 68 – *...the Holy Spirit.*: Acts 10, 17-44

p. 70 – *...intermediate stage of circumcision.*: Acts 10, 45-48

p. 70 – *...house of Israel...*: Mt 10, 5

p. 70 – *...to them alone.*: Mt 15, 24

p. 71 – *...give him accommodation.*: Lk 10, 29-37

p. 71 – *...faith like this.*: Lk 7, 9

p. 72 – *...seven deacons.*: Acts 6, 1-6

p. 72 – *...a missionary tour.*: Acts 14, 1-3

p. 72 – *...Council of Jerusalem.*: Acts 15, 12

p. 72 – *...sent out the Twelve...*: Lk 9, 1-6

p. 72 – *...instructions as the apostles.*: Lk 10, 1-24

p. 73 – *...Jewish symbolism of the time.*: T. Scott, 'Remarks on the universal symbolism of the number 72', *Eye of the Heart: A Journal of Traditional Wisdom*, 1 (2008) pp. 119-140; T. Major, 'The Number Seventy-Two: Biblical and Hellenistic Beginnings to the Early Middle Ages', *Sacris Erudiri* 52 (2013) pp. 7-45.

Chapter 6. Women in the Gospel of Luke

p. 75 – ...*Elizabeth*...: Lk 1, 5-45

p. 75 – ...*the prophetess Anna*...: Lk 2, 36-38

p. 75 – ...*the widow of Naim*...: Lk 7, 11-17

p. 75 – ...*ministered unto Jesus*...: Lk 8, 1-3

p. 75 – ...*bent over*...: Lk 13, 38-42

p. 75 – ...*women of Jerusalem.*: Lk 23, 27-31

p. 75 – ...*lost her coin*...: Lk 15, 8-10

p. 75 – ...*the tenacious widow.*: Lk 18, 1-8

p. 76 – ...*Mary Magdalene*...: Lk 7, 36-50

p. 76 – ...*Mary and Martha*...: Lk 10, 38-42

p. 76 – ...*coins in the temple.*: Lk 21, 1-4

p. 76 – ...*problems in the Church.*: 1 Cor 1, 11

p. 76 – ...*our fellow-Christian.*: Rom 16, 1-2

p. 76 – ...*local community met*...: Acts 16, 14-15

p. 76 – ...*cause of the Gospel.*: Phil 4, 2-3

p. 76 – ...*sufferings and cross.*: Lk 23, 49

p. 78 – ...*their own resources.*: Lk 8, 1-3

p. 78 – ...*liberation of Jerusalem*...: Lk 2, 36-38

p. 79 – ...*Elizabeth had conceived.*: Lk 1, 35-36

p. 79 – ...*filled with the Holy Spirit*...: Lk 1, 41

p. 80 – *...the order of grace.*: 'Dogmatic Constitution on the Church' § 61, *Vatican Council II*, ed. A. Flannery, Dublin 1975, p. 418.

p. 80 – *...Jesus as Messiah.*: 'Dogmatic Constitution on the Church' § 57-58; ib. pp. 416-417.

p. 81 – *...helped at his burial...*: Lk 23: 49, 55-56

p. 81 – *...Easter morning.*: Lk 24, 1-11

p. 81 – *Mary of Magdala as Apostle*: She fulfilled all the requirements to replace Judas as an Apostle – all except one: she was not a man. Peter said the candidate had to be "someone who has been with us the whole time that the Lord Jesus was traveling around with us, someone who was with us right from the time when John was baptising until the day when he was taken up from us – and who can act with us as a witness to his resurrection." (Acts 1, 21-22)

p. 81 – *...Pharisee's house.*: Lk 7, 36-50

Chapter 7. Christ's new priesthood

p. 87 – *...through special prayers.*: Congregation for Divine Worship, *The General Instruction of the Roman Missal* 5th edition, 20 April 2000; J. Wijngaards, 'Don't cage the sacred', *The Tablet*, 23 September 2000, pp 1256-1257.

p. 88 – *...sacred on that account.*: E. Durkheim, *The elementary forms of Religious Life* (1912), ed. and trans. by K. E. Fields, The Free Press, New York 1995; M. Eliade, *Traité d'Histoire des Religions*, Payot, Paris 1959.

p. 89 – *...only in the temple...*: Dt 12, 1-14

p. 89 – *...once a year.*: Heb 9, 7

p. 89 – *...in truth...*: Jn 4, 20-24

p. 89 – *...part of the world.*: Jn 2, 21

p. 89 – *...an ordinary house.*: Mk 14, 12-16

p. 89 – *...hill of execution.*: Heb 14, 12

p. 89 – *...top to bottom.*: Mk 15, 37

p. 90 – *...ears of corn...*: Mt 12, 1-8

p. 90 – *...in the synagogue...*: Mk 13, 6

p. 90 – *...man who had dropsy...*: Lk 14, 1-6

p. 90 – *...man at Siloam.*: Jn 9, 1-16

p. 90 – *...for the sabbath.*: Mk 2, 27

p. 90 – *...his all-sufficient sacrifice.*: Heb 9, 25-28

p. 90 – *...had become meaningless.*: Gal 4, 8-11

p. 91 – *...rose on that day...*: Jn 20, 1

p. 91 – *...indestructible life.*: Heb 7, 16

p. 91 – *...priesthood of the Old Testament.*: Heb 5, 1-4; 7, 26-28

p. 92 – *...her own cross...*: Mt 6, 24

p. 92 – *...persecution and death.*: Mt 10, 16-22

p. 92 – *...priesthood of Christ.*: 1 Pet 2, 5-9

p. 92 – *...God and Father...*: Rev 1, 6

p. 92 – *...God and of Christ.*: Rev 20, 6

p. 92 – *...priesthood to our God.*: Rev 5, 10

p. 93 – *...initiation for women.*: Gen 17, 9-14

p. 93 – *...union with Christ Jesus.*: Gal 3, 26-28

p. 94 – *...priesthood of Christ.*: 'Dogmatic Constitution on the Church', no. 10; *Vatican Council* II, ed. A. Flannery, Dublin 1975, p. 361.

p. 94 – *...Body of Christ.*: 'Dogmatic Constitution on the Church', no. 30; ib. p. 389.

p. 95 – *...remains a man...*: Pope Paul VI, *Inter Insigniores* §27.

p. 96 – *...true image of God.*: Bonaventure, *Quartum Librum*

Sententiarum dist. 25, a. 2, qu. I; *Omnia Opera*, ed. Quaracchi 1889, vol. IV, pp. 649-55. Cf V. E. Hannon, o.c. *The Question of Women and the Priesthood*, London 1967, p. 37.

p. 96 – *...incomplete man...*: '*Femina est mas occasionatus*', i.e. the female is the result of a defect in propagation; Aristotle, *De Generatione Animalium*, II 3; Thomas, *Summa Theol.* I qu. 92, art II; ibid. qu. 99, art 2 ad 1.

p. 96 – *...eminence of degree...*: Thomas Aquinas, *Summa Theologica*, III Suppl., Q. 39, art 1; English transl. Burns and Oates, London 1922, vol. Third Part Q. 34-68, pg 52.

p. 96 – *...he created them.*: Gen 2, 27

p. 96 – *...put on Christ.*: Gal 2, 27

p. 96 – *...who is Spirit.*: 2 Cor 3, 18

p. 97 – *...called by God.*: Heb 5, 4

p. 97 – *...who are tempted.*: Heb 2, 18

p. 97 – *...people's weaknesses.*: Heb 4, 14-16

p. 97 – *...ignorant and the wayward.*: Heb 5, 1-10

p. 97 – *...ruled by its own laws.*: Heb 7, 11-12

p. 97 – *...ruled by its own laws.*: J. M. Ford, 'Biblical Material relevant to the Ordination of Women', *Journal of Ecumenical Studies* 10 (1973), pp. 669-94; synopsised in *Theology Digest* 22 (1974) pp. 23-28.

p. 97 – *...proved his love.*: Jn 15, 12-13

p. 97 – *...distinguished from the hireling.*: Jn 10, 11-15

p. 97 – *...be like Jesus.*: Mt 20, 24-28

p. 97 – *...the Master recognised.*: Jn 13, 12-16

p. 97 – *...you are my disciples.*: Jn 13, 35

p. 98 – *...the apostolic commission.*: Jn 21, 15-17

Chapter 8. The empowerment of women to preside at the Eucharist

p. 100 – *...tax collectors and sinners...*: Mk 2,15-16

p. 100 – *...flask of ointment.*: Mk 14, 3

p. 100 – *...at Jesus' feet.*: Lk 10, 38–42

p. 100 – *...at Jesus' feet.*: "Among the participants at the meal are Lazarus and his sisters", X. Léon-Dufour, *Lecture de l'Évangile selon Jean*, Seuil, Paris, vol. II, p. 443.

p. 101 – *...stipulated by Peter.*: Acts 1, 21-22

p. 101 – *...Eucharist in their home...*: Lk 24, 12-35

p. 101 – *...under Jesus's cross.*: Jn 19, 25

p. 101 – *...under Jesus's cross.*: B. Metzger, *New Testament Studies: Philological, Versional, and Patristic*, Brill, Leiden 1980, pp. 40-41; C. Thiede, *The Emmaus Mystery: Discovering Evidence for the Risen Christ*, A&C Black, London 2006, pp. 94-96.

p. 101 – *...Jewish Passover meals.*: 14 parallels are listed by J. Jeremias, *The Eucharistic Words of Jesus*, 3rd ed., SCM Press, London 1966, esp. pp. 42-61.

p. 101 – *...it was a Passover meal*: This seems confirmed by John's Gospel (Jn 19, 41). Read about this discussion in the *Jewish Quarterly Review*, New Series 42 (1951/52): P. J. Heawood, 'The Time of the Last Supper', pp. 37-44; S Zeitlin, 'The Time of the Passover meal', pp. 45-50. D. Dormeyer, *Die Passion als Verhaltensmodell*, Münster 1947, pp. 88-94; R. Pesch, *Das Markusevangelium*, Vol II, Herder, Freiburg 1977, pp. 340-345; A. J. Kostenberger, 'Was the Last Supper a Passover Meal?' in *The Lord's Supper: Remembering and Proclaiming Christ Until He Comes*, ed. Th. R. Schreiner and M. R. Crawford, Academic, Nashville 2010, pp. 6-30.

p. 101 – *...eat this Passover with you.*": Lk 22, 15. There is convincing evidence to show two ways of calculating the

Passover day were followed in Jesus' time. See A. Jaubert. *La date de la Cène. Calendrier biblique et liturgie chrétienne*, Gabalda & Gle, Paris 1957; C. J. Humphreys, *The Mystery of the Last Supper*, Cambridge University Press 2011; W. Telford, 'Review of The Mystery of the Last Supper: Reconstructing the Final Days of Jesus', *The Journal of Theological Studies* 66 (2015) pp. 371-76.

p. 102 – *...the women and children.":* Mt 14, 21. Compare this to Mark who tells us that, at the multiplication of the loaves, the beneficiaries "numbered about five thousand" (Mk 6,44). Mark just assumes that we realise that apart from the 5,000 men, women and children also were present.

p. 102 – *...daughters and grandmothers.:* Ex 12, 1-11

p. 102 – *...memorial of me.:* See Mt 26, 26-29; Mk 14, 12-16; Lk 22, 17-13; 1 Cor 11, 23-2

p. 103 – *...his disciples, saying....:* Mt 26, 26

p. 103 – *...all disciples who were present.:* It is incorrect to claim, as some scholars do, that Jesus distinguished the two elements: that he allowed all disciples to consume the consecrated bread and wine, but commissioned only the Twelve to perform the consecration. For Jesus, Eucharist and Communion are inseparably intertwined. The Eucharist is one totality, *a memorial meal.* Jesus empowered all his disciples to celebrate it.

This interpretation is strongly affirmed by St Paul. His comments on the Eucharist are the oldest in the New Testament writings. They can be dated to about 50 AD, only 20 years after the Last Supper took place. Paul links both the act of consecrating and the eating and drinking of the consecrated bread and wine to the one act of remembering Jesus: "The Lord Jesus took some bread... saying 'This is my body which is for you; do this as a memorial for me.' In the same way he took the cup after supper, saying 'this cup is the new covenant in my blood. *Whenever you drink it, do this in memory of me.*' Until the Lord comes therefore, every time you eat this bread and drink of this cup, you are proclaiming his death." (1 Cor 11, 23-27).

p. 103 - *...apostles and disciples.*: Ambrose, *On the Mysteries and the Treatise on the Sacraments*, trans. T. Thompson, Macmillan, New York 1919; H. Chadwick (ed.), *Saint Ambrose: on the Sacraments*, book 4, Mowbray, London 1960; M. Reiley Maguire, 'Bible, liturgy concur: women were there', *National Catholic Reporter*, 5 June 1998.

p. 104 - *...an accentuation and specification of baptism.*: E. Schillebeeckx, *Ministry: Leadership in the Community of Jesus Christ*, Crossroad, New York 1981; *The Church with a human face*, SCM, London 1985; R. Schreiter & M. C. Hilkert, *The Praxis of Christian Experience. An Introduction to the Theology of Edward Schillebeeckx*, Harper & Row, San Francisco 1989; J. N. Collins, *Are all Christians ministers?*, Dwyer, Newtown 1992.

p. 104 - *...Congregation for Doctrine.*: Cardinal Joseph Ratzinger, 'Letter to Father Edward Schillebeeckx (June 13, 1984)', *Acta Apostolicae Sedis* 77 (1985) pp. 994-997.

p. 104 - *...May of 1991.*: A. Henderson, *The Killing of Sister McCormack*, HarperCollins, Sydney 2002.

p. 105 - *...before her death.*: 'Do This in Memory of Me', *Compass Theology Review* 25 (1991) no. 4, pp. 33-35.

Chapter 9. Women deacons of the past

p. 107 - *...in the sacristy.*: P. Hünermann, 'Stellungnahme zu den Anmerkungen von Professor Otto Semmelroth SJ betreffend Votum der Synode zum Weihediakonat der Frau', *Diaconia Christi* 10, no. 1 (1975) 33-38; A. Ch. Lochmann, *Studien zum Diakonat der Frau*, Siegen 1996, pp. 167, 189-190.

p. 108 - *...ancient Christian communities.*: G. Otranto, 'Notes on the Female Priesthood in Antiquity', *Journal of Feminist Studies* 7 (1991) pp. 73 - 94; F. Bovon, 'Women Priestesses in the

Apocryphal Acts of Philip', in *New Testament and Christian Apocrypha*, ed. G. Snyder, Baker Academic, Grand Rapids 2009, pp. 246-258; A. Kateusz, *Mary and Early Christian Women. Hidden Leadership*, Palgrave Macmillan 2019.

p. 109 – ...*the venerable mysteries.*: Novella 6, § 3, in R. Schoell and G. Kroll (eds), *Corpus Juris Civilis*, vol III, Novellae, Berlin 1899, p. 43.

p. 109 – ...*by a man.*: Didasc. 16. § 2-3, in G. Homer, *The Didascalia Apostolorum*, Oxford 1929; see also Epiphanius of Salamis in Cyprus (315 - 403), *Against Heresies* c. 79, Migne, *Patrologia Graeca*, vol. 42, cols 744-745.

p. 110 – ...*second birth.*: Ecclesiastical Canons of the Holy Apostles, can. 19; Ch. Hefele, *History of Christian Councils*, Clerk, Edinburgh 1883, vol. I. pp. 450.

p. 111 – ...*third immersion.*: Didascalia 16 § 3; *Apostolic Constitutions* 3,15 (4th cent.); also G. Dietrich, *Die nestorianische Taufliturgie*, 'Ordo baptismi of Ishô'yabh III', Giessen 1903, pp. 96–99.

p. 111 – ...*the baptism.*: The Syriac Book of the Fathers tells us: "Deaconesses perform the sacrament of baptism for women because it is not right for the priest to see the nakedness of women. That is why the deaconesses anoint the women and baptise them in water. The priest should stretch his hand through a window or through a veil to sign the candidates, while the deaconess should perform both the anointing and the baptism itself". I. M. Vosté, *Liber Patrum, Codificazione canonica Orientale*. Fonti, ser. 2, no. 16, Vatican 1940, p. 34.

p. 112 – ...*ordained as minister....*: F.C. Conybeare and O. Wardrop, 'The Georgian Version of the Liturgy of St. James', *Revue de l'Orient chrétien* 19 (1914) pp. 23-33.

p. 113 – ...*the fifth century.*: I outline the complex process of reconstructing the original exemplar more fully in J. Wijngaards, *The Ordained Women Deacons of the Church's first millennium*, Canterbury Press 2011, pp. 20-31.

p. 114 – *...model for the men...*: Acts 6, 5-14

p. 114 – *...one for women.*: Rom 16, 1-2

p. 115 – *...pain of excommunication.*: The Synod of Laodicea (363 AD), Can. 22 & 23; Ch. J. Hefele and H. Leclercq, *Histoire des conciles d'après les documents originaux*, vol. I/2, Paris 1907, p. 1012.

p. 115 – *...priests and deacons.*: '*Lumen Gentium*' § 28; W. M. Abbott (ed.), *The Documents of Vatican II*, New York 1966, pp. 53.

pp. 115-116 – *Genuine sacramental ordination of women:* The ordinations of male and female deacons were virtually identical. If the women were not sacramentally ordained, neither were the men. This is also the considered opinion of the Orthodox scholar and bishop Kallistos Ware. "In the Byzantine rite the liturgical office for laying-on of hands for the deaconess is exactly parallel to that for the deacon; and so, on the principle *lex orandi, lex credendi* – the Church's worshipping practice is a sure indication of its faith – it follows that the deaconess receives, as does the deacon, a genuine sacramental ordination.

K. Ware, 'Man, Woman and the Priesthood of Christ', in Th. Hopko (ed.), *Women and the Priesthood*, New York, 1983, pp. 9-37, here p. 16.

p. 116 – *...the sacramental priesthood.*: D. Ansorge, '*Der Diakonat der Frau. Zum gegenwärtigen Forschungsstand*', in T. Berger/A. Gerhards (ed.), *Liturgie und Frauenfrage*, St. Odilien 1990, 31-65; here p. 60; see also: H. Hoping, '*Diakonat der Frau ohne Frauenpriestertum?*', *Schweizerische Kirchenzeitung* 18 (2000) 14 June; H. Jorissen, '*Theologische Bedenken gegen die Diakonatsweihe von Frauen*', in *Ein Amt für Frauen in der Kirche - Ein frauengerechtes Amt?*', Ostfildern 1997, pp. 86-97; here p. 95; Ch. M. Wilson, review of *The Canonical Implications of*

Ordaining Women to the Permanent Diaconate, by the Canon
Law Society of America, www.ewtn.com, library 1995.

Chapter 10. The Catholic *sense of faith*

p. 117 - *...life of the Church.*: See for instance Clement of
Alexandria, *Stromata* Book 6, chap. 15, 131,4-5; Nicephorus
of Constantinople, *Antirrheticus*, III, 7; Augustine, *De Spiritu
et Littera* 14,23 and 17,30; Thomas Aquinas, *Summa Theologica*
I-II, qu. 106, art. 2. See ST I-II, qu. 106, art. 1, sed cont.; art.
2, ad 3; ST III, qu. 42, art. 4, ad 2; qu. 72, art. 11.

p. 118 - *...ministerial priests.*: These concepts have been worked
out beautifully by the Catholic theologians of Tübingen. J.R.
Geiselmann, *Lebendiger Glaube aus geheiligter Überlieferung*,
Mainz 1942; *Die lebendige Überlieferung als Norm des christlichen
Glaubens*, Freiburg 1959; *Geist des Christentums und des
Katholizismus*, Mainz 1940.

p. 118 - *...the ordination of women.*: B. Knoll & C. J. Bolin, *She
Preached the Word: Women's Ordination in Modern America*,
Oxford University Press 2018.

p. 119 - *...by the hierarchy.*: Spanish language network *Univision*,
19 February 2014.

p. 119 - *...parish councilors.*: T. Bernts en J. Peters 1999. *Dichtbij
en veraf. Het katholieke kader, de katholieken en hun kerk op de
drempel van de 21e eeuw*, KRO, Hilversum 1999.

p. 120 - *...the Holy One...*: 1 John 2, 20.27

p. 120 - *...Word of God.*: 1 Thessalonians 2, 13

p. 120 - *...thoroughly to life.*: Vatican II, 'Lumen Gentium', no. 12;
ed. A. Flannery, Costello, New York 1988, p. 363.

p. 121 - *...contrary to Tradition.*: Vatican II, *Acta synodalia* III/1,
pp. 198-199. The significance of this Council decision is well
explained by R. Gaillardetz, *Teaching with Authority: A Theology
of the Magisterium in the Church*, Liturgical Press 1997, p. 154.

p. 121 – *...faithful souls.*: John Henry Newman, *"The Theory of Developments in Religious Doctrine, 1843"*, reproduced in John Henry Newman, *Conscience, Concensus and the Development of Doctrine: Revolutionary Texts by John Henry Cardinal Newman*, ed. James Gaffney, Image/Doubleday, New York 1992, pp. 6-30.

p. 123 – *...devotional phenomenon:* Extensive documentation can be found in R. Laurentin, *Maria, Ecclesia, Sacerdotium, Nouvelles Éditions Latines*, Paris 1952; much of this material has been translated by me into English and published online. Start from here: http://www.womenpriests.org/why-must-mary-be-considered-a-priest/.

p. 123 – *...salvation of the world.*: St. Antoninus of Florence (1389 - 1459), *Summa Theologica Moralis*, IV, Tit. 15, c. 3, § 3.

p. 123 – *...most holy Eucharist.*: Ferdinand Chirino de Salazar (1575 - 1646 AD), *Canticum*, vol. 2, pp. 92, 94-95.

p. 123 – *...mount of Calvary....*: Bishop Morelle, *Troisième congrès marial breton*, Saint-Brieuc 1911, pp. xiv-xvi.

p. 124 – *...in priestly vestments.*: L. Laplace, *La Mère Marie de Jésus*, Paris 1906, p. 404.

p. 124 – *...according to the Spirit.*: I. Marracci, *Sacerdotium Mysticum Marianum* (ca.1647), passim.

p. 124 – *...Holy Spirit himself.*: F. Maupied, *Orateurs Sacrés*, Paris 1866, vol. 86, p. 228.

p. 124 – *...fullness of grace.*: J-J. Olier (1608 - 1657), *Recueil*, manuscript in Saint Sulpice, Paris, Rue du Regard, p. 230.

p. 124 – *...the Virgin Priest.*: Pius X, *Acta Sanctae Sedis* 9 May 1906; Benedict XV, *Acta Apostolicae Sedis* 8 (1916) p. 146; Pius XI, *Palestra del Clero* 6 (1927) p. 611.

p. 125 – *...the Holy One...*: 1 John 2: 20, 27

p. 125 – *...People as a whole.*: Vatican II, *Lumen Gentium*, no. 12; ed. W. A. Abbott, Guild Press, New York 1966, p. 29.

Chapter 11. The Church's error in condoning slavery

p. 128 – ...*on people's shoulders.*: Mt 23, 4

p. 128 – ...*in certain cases...*: Ex 21, 2-11; 21, 26-27; Dt 23, 16-17

p. 128 – ...*number of circumstances.*: Lev 25, 39-46; Ex 21, 2; Jer 34, 14

p. 129 – ...*treat their slaves...*: Sir 33, 24-31

p. 129 – ...*disposition of God himself...*: Sir 33, 7- 15

p. 129 – ...*not at home.*: Lk 12, 42-48

p. 129 – ...*they are unfair.*: 1 Pet 2, 18-20

p. 129 – ...*obedient to Christ.*: Eph 6, 5-8; 1 Tim 6, 1-2; Titus 2, 9- 10

p. 130 – ...*form of a slave.*: Phil 2,7

p. 131 – ...*a beloved brother.*: Letter to Philemon 16

p. 131 – ...*one in Christ.*: Gal 3, 27-28

p. 132 – ...*brute animals.*: Gregory of Nyssa, *Ecclesiastes*, Hom.4; MIGNE, *Greek Fathers*, Vol.44, 549-550. Gregory adduces many other arguments: how slaves can be seen to be equal to their masters as human beings; what price could ever buy human freedom; etc. etc.

p. 132 – ...*to their cries.*: The Fourth Council of Toledo (633 AD), the Ninth Council of Toledo (655 AD), the Council of Pavia (1012 AD), the Synod of Melfi (1089 AD).

p. 132 – ...*personal sin!*: Thomas Aquinas, *In II Sententiarum* div. 44, qu. l, art.3; *In III Sententiarum* div. 36, qu. l, art. 1 and art. 1, ad 2; *Summa Theologica* I- II, qu. 94, art.5, ad 3; II-II, qu. 57, art. 3, ad 2; *Summa Theologica* III, Suppl. qu. 52, art. 4.

p. 133 – ...*we love ourselves?*: Bartolomé de las Casas, *Unas Avisos y Reglas*, etc.; *El Indio Esclavo; Disputa o controversia con Ginés de Sepúlveda*; all three books at Sevilla in 1552; reprinted at Madrid in 1958.

p. 133 – *...such was tolerated.*: Slavery existed in the Papal States until the end of the 18th century. Slaves were kept in some ecclesiastical institutions as late as 1864. Extensive background material through the centuries is provided by J. F. Maxwell, 'The Development of Catholic Doctrine concerning Slavery', *World Justice* 11 (1969-70) pp. 147-192; 291- 324; *Slavery and the Catholic Church*, Chichester 1975.

p. 134 – *...exchanged or given....*: Instruction by the Holy Office, 20 June 1866.

p. 134 – *...honour of the Creator.*: 'The Church in the Modern World', no. 27; *Vatican Council II*, ed. A. Flannery, o.c. , pg. 928.

Chapter 12. Jesus wants women in the priesthood

p. 138 – *...Spirit of Truth....*: John 14, 16-17. In the original Greek the Spirit is neutral (pneuma). In English I translate the Spirit as a 'he' rather than an impersonal 'it'.

p. 138 – *...said to you.*: John 14, 25-26.

p. 139 – *...lie in the future.*: John 16, 12-14.

p. 140 – *...the Church today?*: Open Letter to John Paul II, 31 October 1994. Full text here: www.womencanbepriests.org/teaching/indiarel.asp.

p. 141 – *...God would be credible.*: *We need you*, 18 August 2002. The 22 Catholic and 5 Protestant signatories of this letter were members of Malaysian Women in Ministry and Theology (MWMT), the Asian Women's Resource Centre for Culture and Theology (AWRC), Empowerment, All Women's Action Society (AWAS) and Basic Ecclesial Communities (BEC). Full text here: www.womencanbepriests.org/care/malay.asp.

p. 142 – *...did not exist.*: G. Heinzelmann, *Die geheiligte Diskriminierung. Beitrage zum kirchlichen Feminismus*, Interfeminas Verlag, Bonstetten 1996.

p. 143 – ...*his sacrifice*.: Sr Vallin, '*Dans les Églises, des Femmes aussi sont ministres*' ('In church communities, women too are ministers'), *Actes du Seminaire, Femmes et Hommes en Église*, Paris 1996, pp. 82-85.

Appendix 1. Papal documents opposing the ordination of women

p. 145 – ...*the ministerial priesthood*.: *Acta Apostolicae Sedis 55* (1976) pp. 267-268; *Briefing 7* (1977) no. 5 & 6.

p. 146 – ...*Doctrine of the Faith*.: *Acta Apostolicae Sedis 69* (1977) pp. 98-116; *L'Osservatore Romano*, Thursday 27 January 1977.

p. 147 – ...*in the church assembly*.: 1 Cor 14, 34-35; 1 Tim 2, 12

p. 147 – ...*veil on the head*.: 1 Cor 11, 2-16

p. 148 – ...*Dignity and Vocation of Women*.: *Acta Apostolicae Sedis* 80 (1988) p. 1715; *On the Dignity of Women*, Pauline Books, Boston 1999.

p. 149 – ...*remembrance of me...*: Lk 22,19; 1 Cor 11,24

p. 149 – ...*retain are retained*.: Jn 20,23

p. 149 – ...*Church as his Bride*.: Eph 5, 25-32

p. 149 – ...*the Church as his Bride*.: H. U. von Balthasar, *Elucidations*, trans. John Riches, London 1975, p. 150 and *Wer ist Kirche? Vier Skizzen*, Freiburg 1965, p. 24.

p. 150 – ...*John Paul II's reflections*.: See, for instance, D. Coffey, 'Priestly Representation and Women's Ordination', in *Priesthood. The Hard Questions* ed. G. P. Gleeson, Dublin 1993, pp. 79-99; J. Manning, *Is the Pope Catholic? A Woman confronts her Church*, Malcolm Lester Books, Toronto, 1999; S. A. Ross, *Extravagant Affections: A Feminist Sacramental Theology*, Continuum, New York 1998, 97-136; "Can God Be a Bride? Some Problems with an Ancient Metaphor", *America* 191 (November 1, 2004) 12-15; also T. Beattie, "Carnal Love and Spiritual Imagination: Can Luce Irigaray and John Paul II Come Together?" in *Sex These Days: Essays on Theology, Sexuality, and Society*, ed. J. Davies and G. Loughlin, Sheffield Academic, Sheffield 1997, 160-83, p. 174; *God's Mother, Eve's Advocate. A Gynocentric Refiguration of Marian Symbolism in Engagement with Luce Irigaray*, Bristol 1999, p. 64.

p. 150 – ...*Pope Benedict XIV or Pope Francis.*: On 29 May 2018 Archbishop Luis Ladaria, Prefect of the Congregation for Doctrine, wrote an article in the *Osservatore Romano* reviving John Paul II's hypothesis. See J. Wijngaards, 'Are women substantially incompatible for the priesthood?', *National Catholic Reporter* 18 June 2018.

p. 150 – ...*Reserving Priestly Ordination to Men Alone.*: Origins 24 (1994) June 9; *L'Osservatore Romano* 24 November 1994.

p. 150 – ...*confirming the brethren...*: cf. Lk 22, 32

p. 151 – ...*Doctrine of the Faith.*: Origins 25 (1995) November 30.

p. 151 – ...*Code of Canon Law.*: L'Osservatore Romano 15 July 1998; Origins 28 (1998) 16 July.

p. 151 – ...*Doctrine of the Faith.*: L'Osservatore Romano 15 July 1998.

p. 152 – ...*November 2, 2002.*: CRONICA, *El Mundo*, Sunday 3 November 2002, no. 368.

p. 152 – ...*May 30, 2008.*: L'Osservatore Romano, 30 May 2008.

p. 152 – ...*documents can be found online.*: For the full online texts of all these documents, see http://www.womenpriests.org/church/rome_wom.asp.

Appendix 3. Genetic basis of gender roles

p. 162 – ...*society rather than other ones.*: F. J. J. Buytendijk, *De Vrouw*, Utrecht 1961, pp. 81 ff; 162-64.

p. 162 – ...*empathy and self-regulation.*: 'Is left frontal brain activation in defensiveness gender specific?', *Journal of*

Abnormal Psychology 107 (1998) pp. 149-153; 'Brain activation during human navigation: gender-different neural networks as substrate of performance', *Nature Neuroscience 3* (2000) pp. 404-408; 'Gender differences in the functional organization of the brain for working memory', *NeuroReport 11* (2000) pp. 2581-2585; 'Gender differences in brain networks supporting empathy', *Neural Image 42* (2008) pp. 393-403; 'Early gender differences in self-regulation and academic achievement', *Journal of Educational Psychology 101* (2009) pp. 689-704.

p. 162 – *...aggressiveness of the young adolescent.*: 'Serum androgenic hormones motivate sexual behavior in adolescent boys', *Fertility and Sterility 43* (1985) pp. 90-94; 'Influence of sex steroid hormones on the adolescent brain and behavior: An update', *The Linacre Quarterly 83* (2016) pp. 308–329.

p. 163 – *...men and women.*: R. G. D'Andrade, 'Sex Differences and Cultural Institutions', in *The Development of Sex Differences*, ed. E. E. Maccoby, Tavistock London 1967, pp. 174-204.

Index

About the Author...

JOHN WIJNGAARDS, DD, LSS, is an internationally renowned theologian and Scripture scholar and is the founder of the Wijngaards Institute for Catholic Research, headquartered in London. His is one of the leading voices in the worldwide movement to include women in the Catholic priesthood.

He was a Mill Hill Missionary priest, and from 1964 to 1976 he was stationed in Hyderabad, India. There he taught Scripture to future priests at St. John's Major Seminary, founded a formation center for religious sisters, and co-founded the Catholic Biblical Association of India. Later, he served as vicar general of his Congregation, from 1976 to 1982.

In 1998, he resigned from the priestly ministry because of a conflict of conscience over the Church's refusal to ordain women.

In a prolific writing career that has spanned six decades, he has authored over two dozen books related to spirituality and theology, some 20 booklets and pamphlets, and 10 film scripts. His books include *What They Don't Teach You in Catholic College*, *The Ordination of Women in the Catholic Church* (in 5 languages), *Communicating the Word of God*, and *Experiencing Jesus.*

From 1982 to 2014, he was director of Housetop International Center for Faith Formation in London, which produced video courses and films for adult faith formation. The Center developed into the Wijngaards Institute, which offers online thousands of documents, in 26 languages, related directly or indirectly to the subject of the ordination of women. The Institute maintains a website, www.womenpriests.org, which is said to be "the largest online academic library on this topic in the world."

He is married to Jackie Clackson, a former art teacher, and they reside in Denham, England, a suburb of London.

Inspiring Books
from
Acadian House Publishing

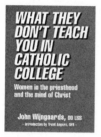

What They Don't Teach You in Catholic College
Women in the priesthood and the mind of Christ

A 216-page hardcover book that makes the case for women in the Catholic priesthood – even though the hierarchy of the Church has traditionally opposed the idea, based largely on their belief that Christ wanted a male-only priesthood for all time. The author, a renowned theologian, disputes that ultra-conservative viewpoint and explains why it is in the Church's best interest to ordain women. (Author: John Wijngaards, DD, LSS. ISBN: 0-9995884-4-3. Price $16.95, hardcover.)

God First
Setting Life's Priorities

A 96-page hardcover book that encourages persons of faith to set priorities, starting with "God first, family second, and everything else third." The book has 10 chapters, with themes that center on gratitude, care for the poor, forgiveness, trusting in God's providence, etc. The chapters are anchored in Scripture and illustrated with inspiring stories from the author's faith journey. (Author: Bryan G. Sibley, M.D. ISBN 0-925417-88-2. Price $14.00)

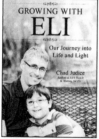

Growing With Eli
Our Journey into Life and Light

Growing With Eli is the third in an inspiring and heartwarming set of books that tell the story of a Lafayette, La., couple and their child, Eli, who was born with a birth defect called *spina bifida*. This volume, published when Eli was 9 years old, tracks the boy's growth from infancy to a healthy, happy youngster. At the same time, on a parallel track, the book chronicles Eli's father's growth in and understanding of his Catholic faith. (Author: Chad Judice. ISBN: 0-9995884-2-7. Price: $17.95, hardcover)

> Book 3 of the internationally recognized "Waiting For Eli" trilogy

Freedom From Fear
A Way Through The Ways of Jesus The Christ

Everyone at one time or another feels fear, guilt, worry and shame. But when these emotions get out of control they can enslave a person, literally taking over his or her life. In this 142-page softcover book, the author suggests that the way out of this bondage is prayer, meditation and faith in God and His promise of salvation. The author points to the parables in the Gospels as Jesus' antidote to fears of various kinds, citing the parables of the prodigal son, the good Samaritan, and the widow and the judge. Exercises at the end of each chapter help make the book's lessons all the more real and useful. (Author: Francis Vanderwall. ISBN: 0-925417-34-3. Price: $14.95)

Dying In God's Hands

A 152-page hardcover book that provides keen insights into the hearts and minds of the dying. It is based on a dozen or more interviews with terminally ill hospice patients, in which they share their hopes, dreams, fears and needs. The majority of the interviews provide evidence that faith in God and belief in the hereafter are the greatest strengths of the dying. Designed to comfort the dying and their loved ones, the book also contains a section of prayers and prose from all major world religions. (Author: Camille Pavy Claibourne. ISBN: 0-925417-64-5. Price: $16.95)

Purses & Shoes For Sale
The Joys and Challenges of Caring for Elderly Parents

A 216-page book about the author's journey as a caregiver to her elderly parents in the twilight of their lives. Packed with suggestions on how to deal with issues encountered by adult children of the elderly. Includes a Q&A section with answers to frequently asked questions, plus a resources section with practical advice, useful websites and glossary of terms. (Author: Camille Pavy Claibourne. Hardcover ISBN: 0-925417-96-3. Price: $17.95; Softcover ISBN: 0-925417-49-1. Price: $14.95)

The Elephant Man
A Study in Human Dignity

The Elephant Man is a 138-page softcover book whose first edition inspired the movie and the Tony Award-winning play by the same name. This fascinating story, which has touched the hearts of readers throughout the world for over a century, is now complete with the publication of this, the Third Edition. Illustrated with photos and drawings of The Elephant Man. (Author: Ashley Montagu. ISBN: 0-925417-41-6. Price: $12.95.)

Getting Over the 4 Hurdles of Life

A 160-page hardcover book that shows us ways to get past the obstacles, or hurdles, that block our path to success, happiness and peace of mind. Four of the most common hurdles are "I can't / You can't," past failures or fear of failure, handicaps, and lack of self-knowledge. This inspiring book – by one of the top motivational speakers in the U.S. – is brought to life by intriguing stories of various people who overcame life's hurdles. Introduction by former LSU and NBA star Shaquille O'Neal. (Author: Coach Dale Brown. ISBN: 0-925417-72-6. Price: $17.95)

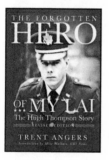

The Forgotten Hero of My Lai
The Hugh Thompson Story (Revised Edition)

The 272-page hardcover book that tells the story of the U.S. Army helicopter pilot who risked his life to rescue South Vietnamese civilians and to put a stop to the My Lai massacre during the Vietnam War in 1968. Revised Edition shows President Nixon initiated the effort to sabotage the My Lai massacre trials so no U.S. soldier would be convicted of a war crime. (Author: Trent Angers. ISBN: 0-925417-90-4. Price: $22.95)

TO ORDER, list the books you wish to purchase along with the corresponding cost of each. For shipping in the U.S., add $4 for the first book, and $1 per book thereafter. For shipping out of the U.S., email us at info@acadianhouse.com for a price quote. Louisiana residents add 9% tax to the cost of the books. Mail your order and check or credit card authorization (VISA/MC/AmEx) to: Acadian House Publishing, P.O. Box 52247, Lafayette, LA 70505. Or call (800) 850-8851. To order online, go to www.acadianhouse.com.